THE CHINESE OVERSEAS
From Earthbound China to the Quest for Autonomy

WANG GUNGWU

Harvard University Press
CAMBRIDGE, MASSACHUSETTS
LONDON, ENGLAND

Copyright © 2000 by the President and
Fellows of Harvard College

All rights reserved

Printed in the United States of America

First Harvard University Press paperback edition, 2002

Library of Congress Cataloging-in-Publication Data
Wang, Gungwu.
The Chinese overseas : from earthbound China to the quest
for autonomy / Wang Gungwu.
p.   cm.
"Edwin O. Reischauer lectures."
Includes bibliographical references and index.
ISBN 0-674-00234-2 (cloth)
ISBN 0-674-00986-X
1. Chinese—Foreign countries—History.   I. Title: From earthbound
China to the quest for autonomy.   II. Title.

DS732.W346 2000   99-053438

To Margaret

Contents

1 Seaward Sweep:
The Chinese in Southeast Asia

1

2 The Sojourners' Way

39

3 The Multicultural Quest for Autonomy

79

Notes	Index
121	143

THE CHINESE OVERSEAS

CHAPTER ONE

Seaward Sweep: The Chinese in Southeast Asia

When I first studied the early trade of the South China Sea, I was struck both by China's contacts in the region as early as the third century B.C. and by the range of possibilities for a growing commercial relationship between China and what looked like a smaller Mediterranean Sea. There were major differences, of course. The sea was more open and more dangerous. The southern and eastern sides were archipelagos rather than another continent. And one empire, China, was dominant, and unchallenged by any maritime power for at least two millennia. Nevertheless the early trade of the first millennium A.D. looked most promising, especially from the Three Kingdoms period (220–280), when the southern kingdom of Wu sought out the Southeast Asian kingdoms and ports for a closer relationship, to the diplomatic and trading relations established during the Tang dynasty (618–906).

The relationship sought by the kingdom of Wu continued to grow. Following the rapid population growth in South China during the second millennium, trade and diplomatic relations gradually became more intense and profitable for both Chinese and various groups of Asian merchants before the arrival of the Europeans in the sixteenth century. But the numbers of Chinese involved in that trade remained relatively small, and few Chinese actually went abroad to live for any length of time. Even more interesting is the fact that, by the time the Chinese did move into the region in large numbers, most of the area had come under Western control.

Why didn't the Chinese take advantage of their early links with the trading ports of Asia? There are many historical questions to examine. They include those concerning the nature of the Chinese imperial state and its policies toward trade, migration, and foreign affairs, and the region's attitudes toward China, but they also touch on specific events, certain cultural values, and the individual's relationship with his family and home. The questions are far-ranging and cover a great variety of issues, large and small. I have chosen here to look at only a few of them.

There are countless clichés about China, and most of them carry a measure of truth. One of the best-known is relevant to the questions asked here; it is the phrase "earthbound China." I shall expand on it a little and put it in historical perspective by saying that "landbound and agrarian" defines China as much as "maritime enterprise" underlines the development of Europe. It is a good place to begin to try to understand the way Chinese people have dealt with maritime Asia and why it took so long for the relationship to overcome its initial constraints and finally prosper. In this chapter, I focus on Southeast Asia, which is where most Chinese who traveled outside China went, eventually living and making their homes there.

The story of China's relations with Southeast Asia has many layers. The phrase earthbound China suggests that the Chinese who went overseas may be seen as atypical, if not downright un-Chinese. It is less well known how the Chinese in Southeast Asia have chafed at that stereotype and striven to prove it wrong. Premodern history helps us to understand the complexity of what occurred.

ORIGINS OF THE CONTINENTAL MIND-SET

For a people whose heartland, when they appeared in history as "Chinese," was the north-central plains of the Yellow River, the maritime world of Southeast Asia was a long way away. In addition, the formation of the Chinese core population required people to move in different directions. During the first and second millennia B.C., various tribal peoples from the north and northwest moved toward the religious and political center located around the bend of the Yellow River and its lower reaches. This area represented the greatest wealth and culture in their known world. The result was the establishment of an ever more powerful polity that thereafter set out to expand outward. By the middle of the first millennium B.C., the center had acquired the intellectual vigor and administrative sophistication that made its power irresistible to the agricultural neighbors to its southeast and southwest. Before the end of that millennium, China had reached the southern coasts and dominated the Yangzi Valley from its delta to the Tibetan foothills.

In sharp contrast, this same polity made little headway toward the lands to the north and west, where the steppes nurtured nomadic tribes that were part of great confederations.[1] Those tribes that migrated inward, however, eventually became Chinese. But for much of three millennia, few Chinese migrated northward or westward. Instead, the rural and trading Chinese moved readily among their eastern and southern neighbors, ultimately filling the wild spaces and deep valleys of their hilly terrains. The progress of these Chinese was stopped only by the East and South China Seas. Along the coasts, over a period of centuries, they met and intermingled with, and then dominated and absorbed, most of the indigenous so-called Hundred Yue peoples.[2] All of the Yue peoples, unlike the north-central families who later moved south to live among them, were native to the wetlands and tropical and subtropical climate, and they developed coastal shipping and traveled inland by the many navigable waterways. The Yue fisher folk by the sea sailed up and down the coasts, most notably between the Shandong peninsula and the Yangzi regions of modern Jiangsu and Zhejiang, and the Pearl and Red River deltas of modern Guangdong and northern Vietnam. But they did not venture further.

In contrast, the ancient peoples of Mesopotamia and Egypt, during their formative years, had easy access to the eastern Mediterranean. Their civilizations stimulated others, which became even more dependent on maritime activity, notably the Phoenicians and the various Greek states. It is inconceivable that the West could have developed as it did without the region's geographical and economic underpinnings that produced the people who appreciated Homer's Trojans and Greeks. In China, there simply was no comparable figure to that of Ulysses in the whole of ancient Chinese folklore, literature, or history. And no ruler of China ever had to cross the sea to save his empire as Julius Caesar had to do. There was no need; the other shore was never where the enemy was.

It is also important to note that Southeast Asia did not develop in a way that attracted much attention from China. State formation in the region was not discernible until the beginning of the first millennium A.D. There were no trading cities or ports that had much to offer their counterparts in Guangzhou and Hanoi (which China controlled for more than a thousand years before the middle of the tenth century A.D.). Not surprisingly, the earliest records of trade with China concern merchants who had come from South Asia and the Middle

East across the Indian Ocean. When northern Chinese migrant families moved south, especially from the fourth century A.D. onward, they adapted to the wetlands and to coastal living, and grew accustomed to many alterations in the elite Huaxia (Chinese) culture they had brought with them. But one elite concern made all the difference for the development of eastern and southern China throughout history: elite dependence on the cultural center in the north, which was characterized by an "earthbound," continental mind-set regarding the nature of imperial Chinese civilization. This perspective served as the fundamental precondition of agrarian power for all Chinese emperors. The centripetal force that tied all parts of China to the successive capitals in the north, whether located in the northwest like Changan, the north-center like Loyang and Kaifeng, or the northeast like Beijing, was enormously powerful. The capital's demands, and the opportunities it had to offer, pulled toward the center the best talents, the richest trade, and indeed all the wealth and resources that the center wanted. It was also this force that was to deny the need for adventures across the seas and inhibited the development of trading and diplomatic relations even after the ports and capitals of Japan and Southeast Asia became increasingly prosperous and attractive to Chinese merchants.

Opportunities for China to expand its relationship with Southeast Asia existed from very early times. We might begin with the record of Xu Fu, sent to the eastern islands (he was thought to have reached Japan) when Qin Shihuangdi was emperor (221–209 B.C.) in search of materials to prolong life. It is astonishing how active the Xu Fu societies in Japan are today in commemorating that first connection. If they are right, the first overseas Chinese settled in Japan late in the third century B.C., and their descendants remain proud to identify with that past.[3]

Later, during the first millennium A.D., from the first century onward, the Han empire and its successors conducted its overseas trade, and the necessary "tributary" diplomacy, from ports much further south, out of Guangzhou (now the provinces of Guangdong, Guangxi, and Hainan) and Jiaozhou (now northern Vietnam). Chinese records reveal numerous kingdoms trading with China, but, except for Funan, Linyi, and Zhenla on the mainland (now Vietnam and Cambodia) and Sri Vijaya and Heling in Java-Sumatra, they were small polities or port cities, which were incapable of challenging China's power. Precise identification of these places has been tenuous. That in itself suggests why the unified central empire of China did not take them very seriously at the time.[4]

Coastal ships had long been available to the Chinese, but the volume of trade did not stimulate an industry for oceangoing vessels. Nor did the state feel the need for an imperial fleet. For several centuries, the majority of the Chinese traders and Buddhist pilgrims heading for, and returning from, India and West Asia via Southeast Asian ports traveled in foreign ships. There were the ships of the *bosi* and *kunlun* peoples from the region itself,[5] and there were also Indian and Persian, and later Arab, vessels.

China certainly had the technology to build oceangoing ships. The evidence of the Zhu Ying and Kang Tai expeditions to Southeast Asia in the third century A.D. shows that the skills were there. These skills were simply not encouraged, however, and therefore remained unexploited.

The many official contacts throughout the fifth and sixth centuries, especially between Buddhist Chinese rulers and their counterparts in Southeast and South

Asia, testify to steady religious, trading, and diplomatic relationships in which many coastal Chinese were involved. These led to a major expansion during the Tang dynasty in the trade in spices and medicinal products, which had repercussions in the island economies of the Malay Archipelago.[6]

During the Tang dynasty (618–907), some officials and court eunuchs were sent abroad on the emperor's, or the provincial governor's, business, including to southern kingdoms on the Korean peninsula and to Japan, but I shall confine myself to those who went to Southeast Asia. It was well known, even taken for granted, that the trade at China's ports, especially that of Guangzhou, provided a profitable business for the officials themselves. At another level, private travel was also known. Many Buddhist priests and scholars left China for India, some never to return, including those who chose to reside at religious centers in Southeast Asia itself. I am tempted to compare some of them to modern Chinese students who travel to the West in search of the Truth and do not return, but must note that the scale was much smaller then, and that the imperial state at the time obviously took little interest in their transfers of technology.[7]

In contrast, the Roman empire and its successors were also continental powers at their peak but never as stable as the major dynasties of the Han (206 B.C.–A.D. 220) or the Tang (618–907) in China. Because the equivalent heartland, whether seen from Rome or from Constantinople, was actually the favored coasts of the Mediterranean, the European states always gave more weight to control of the sea and tried to keep a balanced view of their landward interests. Even when Rome fell and left a military vacuum, this was quickly filled by Muslim-Arab expansions across the whole length of the southern Mediterranean. If we think of the Mediterranean as the equivalent of the North China plains, it is clear that trade and war in the West had to be based on a worldview and power structure totally different from that of China.

Thus the three millennia from the second millennium B.C. to the end of the first millennium A.D. left the differences between the two worlds so entrenched that it is enough to say the Chinese could not possibly have thought or acted like Westerners even when they were in pursuit of similar trading and military objectives.

SWEEPING SOUTH AND PULLING BACK

What of the last thousand years? China fought many overland wars with the mainland Southeast Asian states, and several naval expeditions were sent across the China Seas between the thirteenth and fifteenth centuries. Chinese envoys and other officials were dispatched from time to time in order to affirm the emperor's cosmic and terrestrial superiority. But for the ordinary Chinese, trade would have been the only reason to venture out across the seas and sojourn in foreign parts. It is unclear before the tenth century how many Chinese actually traveled overseas for trade. There are records dating from after the tenth century that describe Chinese traders as having gone out to trade with every intention of returning with their cargo. We can extrapolate from these observations for the earlier periods to say that no Chinese could be described as deliberately leaving, or having left, China permanently before the tenth century. These were not the precursors of the overseas Chinese of the nineteenth and twentieth centuries.

At the fall of the Tang dynasty at the beginning of the tenth century, five territories along the coast were detached from the Chinese heartland. They became kingdoms in their own right (three went further and called themselves "empires"). All were exceptionally well placed to expand their trade with the countries of the South China Sea. They were

- the Nan Tang empire (which contested control of the mouth of the Yangzi River, although its capital was more inland, in Nanjing),
- the Wu Yue kingdom (mainly the province of Zhejiang, with its capital in Hangzhou, but also controlling part of the Yangzi mouth),
- the Min empire (the province of Fujian, capital at Fuzhou),
- the Nan Han empire (which controlled both modern Guangdong and Guangxi provinces, with its capital at Guangzhou), and
- the Nam Viet kingdom (this had been the Protectorate of Annan, in northern Vietnam, with its capital in Hanoi; it alone remained independent after the Song reconquest of the south by 978).

Four of these capitals were located in trading ports, and this facilitated a considerable expansion of overseas trade, if only for the revenues that it could bring. Except for Nam Viet, or Vietnam, the kingdoms lasted between fifty and seventy years.[8]

With spirited effort, and perhaps also with some luck, Vietnam broke clear of Chinese control and started on the long road to what it has become today, a Southeast Asian country. The Chinese traders and officials and their descendants who had settled there earlier, or who chose to remain after the kingdom achieved a precarious independence, became Vietnamese. This development may not seem relevant to developments in the modern era, but it alerts us to questions of sojourning, settlement, and assimilation that have emerged in recent times (see Chapter 2).

In the other four kingdoms, at least two generations of rulers and officials were preoccupied with the problems of survival as coastal states. They knew the value of overseas trade and depended on the profits of that trade to help finance their defense against the continual threat of reunification that would put an end to their independence. In contrast, the emperors of all the earlier dynasties, and almost all the central officials before the twelfth century (that is, before the Southern

Song dynasty, 1127–1279), were born and brought up in landlocked continental China.

The other four kingdoms became fully integrated in the Song empire (the Northern Song dynasty, 960–1126) by the end of the tenth century, and there is little doubt that the tenth century provided a major stimulant to overseas trade. The Song success in reunifying the empire during the two decades after 960, however, returning the center of power to its capital in Kaifeng back in north-central China, slowed down that development. It also ended the best opportunity that the enterprising Chinese of coastal China ever had to develop autonomously if not independently of an earthbound empire. For the next 150 years, the empire's preoccupation was with defending its northern frontiers. But, in 1127, Kaifeng fell to the Jurchen Jin dynasty (1115–1234). The Jurchen came from the Liao Valley in the northeast and comprised partially sinicized tribes, ancestors of the later Manchu. When Kaifeng fell, the Song emperors were forced to move south to Hangzhou, and it is that move that led to the beginning of a new era for the expansion of coastal trade. With Hangzhou, the first imperial capital directly open to the sea was established. This offered the southern Chinese a great opportunity to escape from the earthbound mind-set of the empire that had dominated Chinese history. For the entrepreneurial Chinese along the southern coasts, it stimulated the commercial involvements with Southeast Asia (and Korea and Japan) that, despite interruptions from time to time, were to last till the present day.[9]

The growing Song navy during this period proved that seafaring had become a major profession. The technology to advance Chinese interests overseas was in place. But the Southern Song also made clear that the obstacle to further growth in southern trade was not only the traditional mind-set. Another hindrance was the geopolitics of a continental power. The real threats to the Song came always from the north. The energies and resources needed to reunify with the Chinese heartland, and also to defend the southern dynasty against continuous attacks by the Jurchen during the twelfth century and then the Mongols during the thirteenth, inhibited any initiatives for further trading extensions overseas. It is tantalizing to read Zhao Rugua's *Zhu fan zhi* (completed early in the thirteenth century), with its details of the numerous foreign countries trading with China, to speculate on what might have happened if the Chinese had held off the Mongol armies for the next century.[10] Would that have been long enough to modify the continental mind-set that characterized every central power in China? Could that have unbound the feet of earth-bound China?

The fact remains that the southern Chinese who were engaged in overseas trading only had 150 years of imperial encouragement. The Southern Song capital, Hangzhou, fell to the Mongols in 1278 and the conquest of the whole of China by Kublai Khan returned the imperial capital once again to the north, this time to Beijing, where it remained for all but sixty years of the next seven centuries. As had happened so many times in the past, the southern Chinese had to look northward for direction and were again subjected to northern control. There is no doubt that northern overland and continental concerns dominated.

But all was not lost. Private trade overseas did continue to grow under the reunified Mongol Yuan empire (1278–1368). This trade was largely in the hands of Muslims from Central Asia, Persia, and the Arab world, who were better trusted by the Mongols, but they were joined by many Chinese, and indeed many of these Muslim and other foreign traders themselves stayed on to become Chinese. Thus the impact of foreign commerce on southern China was still considerable. We can see this in the personal experiences of Wang Tayuan, as recorded in his remarkable book, *Daoyi zhilue*, where he recorded his travels for over eight years and where he describes or mentions more than a hundred ports and cities.[11] He writes in the Postface of this work: "China's traders who go forth among the different courts and various territories travel as if between the prefectures of the east and the west."[12] That is, they traded outside China as if they were within different parts of the empire, thus confirming the image of a Pax Mongolica across the oceans as well. For a brief period, the Mongol Yuan was both a continental and a maritime power.

The participation of the traders of the twelfth to fourteenth centuries (the Southern Song and Yuan periods), not necessarily Han Chinese, kept the ocean-going skills of coastal China alive. This trade encouraged the shipping industry to develop further and enabled the first naval expeditions to cross the seas to invade Japan and Java under Kublai Khan at the end of the thirteenth century. And as more southern coastal Chinese came to participate directly in that trade, many began to sojourn in the port cities of the Southeast Asian Mediterranean. There is evidence that, following the fall of the Southern Song, some of the sojourners had established small communities in these locations.[13] With the fall of the Yuan, others, including non-Han Muslim Chinese, settled down to new lives in the region, notably in Champa (central Vietnam), in Cambodian and other ports of the Gulf of Thailand, and in Java and Sumatra. The numbers were not large enough to have invited description, and it can only be assumed that most of those who settled were soon assimilated fully into the local societies.

Despite these outgoing manifestations, we must not read too much into the new awareness of the sea. There was no maritime transformation in the nature of Chinese civilization. The Chinese worldview did not share the idea of a Pax Mongolica. The elites who, under pressure from northern instability and invasions, migrated southward to the coastal provinces during the whole period of the Song dynasty brought with them an even stronger Confucian perspective. They clung loyally to the values and status structures that distinguished them as Chinese from the "barbarians" both north and south. This attitude was further bolstered by southern contributions made to the evolution of Neo-Confucianism, a consolidation of key principles that were strongly rooted in agrarian society and further reinforced by elite loyalties. The people of Fujian, for example, were particularly proud that the great philosopher Zhu Xi was one of them.[14]

Although many of the genealogies of these southern elite families, whether in Guangdong or Fujian, or among latecomers like the Hakka (Kejia) in the hill-lands, may not be authentic, the consistent references in them to their earthbound continental origins reflect the persistence of the dominant north-central mindset.[15] For these elites and their descendants, the Mongol-inspired opportunity to open China to the world was not a blessing. If not quite a disaster for China, it was certainly a departure from the norm, and this was something that the Chinese bearers of Han and Tang civilization were prepared to reject if they had a chance to do so. In trying to adjust to their status as subjects of the Mongols, they reaffirmed with greater determination than ever their identification with their original heritage.

The chance to restore their rightful value system came with the founding of the Ming (1368–1644) dynasty. Founded in central China after driving the Mongols beyond the line where Ming emperors were to build the Great Wall, this was a dynasty of many contradictions where overseas relations were concerned. The founder, Zhu Yuanzhang, had to defeat a great rival who commanded naval power off the eastern coasts. Zhu's subsequent decision to ban private trade with foreign merchants caused much frustration and conflict along the whole coast, and led to the rise of Wako pirates (largely Japanese and Chinese who felt that they had been denied their livelihood in overseas trade). The Ming empire rejected the relatively liberal Mongol policies and reimposed, in a stronger and more institutionalised form, the tributary system that had become desultory and weak for three centuries. In this way Zhu Yuanzhang reaffirmed the tradition that the coastal southern Chinese should look inward and northward again. Paradoxically, during the reign of his son, Zhu Di (better known as the Emperor Yongle), the dynasty produced the great voyages of Zheng He. His ventures into the Indian Ocean in 1405–1433 marked the high point of Chinese naval history.[16]

In contrast, the Afro-Eurasian Mediterranean during the comparable period was divided between Islamic and Christian kingdoms. In addition, the Mongol invasions of Eastern Europe and the Middle East created a new continental force that the Mediterranean states found difficult to contain. Increasingly, the Germanic and Slavic polities adapted to continental standards of trade and war. But Europe was not to be sucked into the geopolitics of the Eurasian heartland. Despite the successes of Venice and Genoa and other city-states, the maritime periphery shifted northward and westward when control of the Mediterranean had to be shared. Again the seas provided the impetus for the next stage of economic and political development. The new maritime peoples of Portugal and Spain, of Britain and the Netherlands, had to turn to the West and South Atlantic for opportunities to seek their fortunes. Eventually, they reached the new world of the Americas traveling in one direction and rounded the Cape of Good Hope into the Indian Ocean in the other.

As islands, Britain's dependence on the sea provided the country with new opportunities; it responded quickly and aggressively. The other three states of Spain, Portugal, and the Netherlands, however, would not have needed to depend on the sea if they had had control over larger chunks of the Continent. They were more like the provinces in China, which could be seen as their equivalents: for example, provinces like Guangdong, Zhejiang, Jiangsu, and Shandong could be compared to Spain and the Netherlands, while Fujian shared a lack of natural resources with Portugal. Given the technology, the trading traditions, and the economic necessity, there should have been nothing to prevent the port peoples of China's southern and coastal provinces from becoming the maritime pioneers of the East Asian world. But when such comparisons are made, the lack of maritime initiatives from any of these provinces is obvious. One must conclude that the constraints of a continental mind-set and the pull of all the institutions established by a powerful political and cultural center in China were what made the difference.

The most striking example of this difference is the decision to stop all maritime expeditions after Zheng He returned from his last voyage in 1433. The ships were put away, the captains and sailors redeployed; eventually the records were destroyed and the story of this great burst of naval power almost forgotten. The coastal peoples were forced to return to the land, and when that could not earn them a livelihood and they had to go to sea, their ships were severely limited in size and capacity. No foreign trade was permitted. Of course, this did not stop the trade altogether. Tribute missions still arrived and some private commerce with the missions was allowed, and there are references to foreign traders' colluding with local officials and merchants despite the ban.

In the sixty years that followed its foundation, Ming policy broke the momentum of Chinese maritime development that had grown steadily since the tenth century. But the commercial possibilities opened up by the Zheng He voyages left a legacy of opportunity for the coastal peoples of South China that bureaucratic prohibitions could not prevent. The brave or desperate few, knowing where the rich cargoes were, continued to trade at great risk to themselves, and the trickle of private enterprise in the interstices of the official tributary trading system seems to have thrived. By the sixteenth century, it was clear that the scale would remain small and the ventures dangerous until and unless new actors came into play. What was needed was a force that would push the Chinese to unbind their feet from their good earth, some external force that the government in Beijing could not control.

The latter part of this period of hiatus in Chinese initiatives, during the first half of the sixteenth century, coincided with a burst of maritime energy from Europe. The Portuguese came to Asia, captured Malacca and, with the help of the Chinese they met there, found their way to the key ports of South China. How they aroused local business interests and defied the officials, and what Beijing tried to do to discourage them, have been well studied. The fact that they went on to Japan in the midst of an extended Japanese civil war and stimulated the trading ambitions of the feudal lords of Kyushu and Kansai was ominous for Ming policy. The restlessness of the coastal merchants of China coincided with this new period of opportunity. The example of the armed fleets of the Portuguese awakened both Chinese and Japanese to action, and fresh Wako organizations grew up to breach the trade bans still in force on the China coast.[17]

Particularly important was the challenge posed to the frustrated Chinese merchants of Guangdong and Fujian by the Portuguese and the Spanish, to be followed later by the Dutch and the English. These were the descendants of the generations of active participants in the Southeast Asian and Indian Ocean trade during the Song and Yuan dynasties. They knew what they could have done if the successor empire of the Ming dynasty had not clamped down on their enterprises. While many had turned their creative energies to serve the stable agrarian communities they lived among, many others, including less earthbound relatives who were less steeped in the dominant Neo-Confucian values, saw no contradiction between agrarian virtues and an active foreign trade. Indeed, throughout the empire, a more favorable disposition toward trade had been developing since the twelfth century, and traditional mandarin prejudice against merchants had been tempered by the economic value to the empire of their entrepreneurial activities. While the Ming rulers after the fourteenth century insisted that the new disposition did not apply to private trade with the outside world, there was a significant change in attitude that some elite families were prepared to take advantage of.

The changes were accentuated by the arrival of aggressive and well-organized trading organizations from Europe, all backed by their governments to a greater or lesser extent. They were further stimulated by the enthusiastic response of Chinese and Japanese adventurers who also had links with their respective local powerful families. The stage was therefore set for a new push for the relaxation of private foreign trade. By the middle of the sixteenth century, the mandarins who administered the trading bans on the China coast discovered how unworkable these had become. The Wako threats to the Yangzi Delta spread south to Fujian and Guangdong. The defense system was totally inadequate and the coastal areas were in an uproar.

A two-pronged response eventually brought relative peace: major military counterattacks plus a relaxation of the trading prohibitions. The grudging reluctance to admit the failure of the prohibitionist policy of the Ming dynasty can be seen in the way these two methods have been treated in official records. The former, the military solution, was fully chronicled, and the many heroic efforts to defend the coasts were well rewarded. In contrast, the equally important easing of the prohibitions against trading contacts with foreigners who came by sea received little attention. The officials who implemented the trading ban faithfully were blamed for causing the unrest along the coast. But there was no change in official policy, no appreciation that important new forces had arrived at the doors of China, only the minor modifications thought to be necessary to bring peace to the region. A good illustration of this lack of a fresh assessment may be seen in the informal, almost surreptitious, agreement by provincial authorities in Guangdong to let the Portuguese use Macau as a trading base. When the Portuguese left Macau in 1999, they had had some 450 years of marginal and shallow, but continuous, contact with China.

The easing of the ban had considerable impact on the people of South China. Although the Wako pirates and other bands of smugglers and illicit traders were crushed, their skills in organizing fleets of armed trading vessels to conduct the trade of Southeast Asia were not lost. On the contrary, they laid the foundations for the maritime power that three generations of the Zheng family (Zheng Zhilong, Zheng Chenggong, and Zheng Jing) were able to build in Fujian and on the island of Taiwan in the seventeenth century. That power was based largely on trade with Southeast Asian kingdoms and ports, often in direct competition with European armed shipping, notably that of the Dutch and the Spanish. The Zheng fleets demonstrated the great potential for both entrepreneurship and maritime superiority at a critical period in Southeast Asian history. The pent-up demands of the coastal provinces were explosive when their energies were released. European records for this period reveal how dynamic the Chinese merchants were, and point to the threat to Western trade that they could have provided, had they not been embroiled in mainland politics when the Manchus conquered Ming China in 1644.

The two decades from the 1620s to the fall of the Ming dynasty in 1644 marked the peak of Chinese free-ranging commercial activity in Southeast Asia before modern times. Three conditions were critical in enabling the Chinese—mainly the southern Fujianese or Hokkiens—to achieve such heights of success.

The first condition was a greatly weakened central government in Beijing, which allowed the coastal provinces to engage in foreign trade. The Ming rulers had been threatened continuously by rebellions and foreign invasion from the end of the sixteenth century: rebellion in the southwest, Hideyoshi's invasion of Korea, the Manchu seizure of its territories in Liaodong, and, the last straw, the peasant uprisings led by Li Zicheng and Zhang Xianzhong. The government was so weak that a series of massacres of Chinese in

Manila and Batavia (now Jakarta) during this period was met by, at best, feeble protests. Already it was clear that, however successful the Chinese were in the Southeast Asian region, it aroused no interest at the center. The grave dangers to regime survival reinforced the deep-rooted continental mind-set.

The second condition was the reduction of Japanese activity in the region in accordance with Tokugawa policy, which left the Chinese with no other Asian rivals. The most successful maritime traders of the earlier centuries, such as the Indians, Persians, and Arabs, had been marginalized by European naval power in the sixteenth century. Native Southeast Asian trading fleets were no match against the Portuguese, Spanish, and Dutch armed ships. Only the Japanese remained as either partners or rivals when Chinese trading power reemerged during the second half of the sixteenth century. With the Japanese withdrawal and their belated adoption of "closed door" policies, the Chinese seaborne trade, relatively free in comparison, flourished without competition among Asian merchants.

The third condition was the fierce rivalry between the Dutch and the Spanish, which gave the Chinese privateers room to maneuver. With Portugal coming under the Spanish crown, the Dutch were forced to become more aggressive in building their own trading networks. Their base in Batavia put them at a disadvantage in the East Asian trade as compared with Macau and Manila, but their acquisition of Taiwan and their successes at Hirado and Nagasaki enabled them to compete. The Chinese merchants operating in Southeast Asia benefited by being able to provide both sides with help in accumulating local goods for long-distance trade to the West. As long as they were no direct threat, these Chinese were invaluable to the expansion of European trade in the region. This factor was to become even more important in the centuries to come.

There are features of these three conditions that may appear familiar when we contemplate more recent developments in the region. I shall come back to them in Chapter 3.

But let me return to the maritime aspirations of the Chinese and the combined force of geopolitics and earthbound tradition from which there was no escape. In 1644 the Ming dynasty was replaced by the Manchu Qing dynasty, overland conquerors who reinstated the overseas bans even more effectively than the previous regime. The reasons why they did so were understandable. As invaders who were outnumbered immensely by hostile Han Chinese throughout the empire, they could allow no opposition, even from the maritime periphery. When that periphery was threatened by the considerable mobile maritime force led by Zheng Chenggong, better known as Koxinga (Lord of the Imperial Surname), in the name of the defeated Ming imperial house, with an offshore base in Taiwan, draconian measures were necessary. These centered on a ruthless decision to move all coastal residents, especially in Fujian and Guangdong, ten or more miles inland, in order to deny the Ming loyalists any local support. This was the first step back to land-bound China.

After the Zheng forces on Taiwan surrendered in 1683, the reaffirmation of the continental mind-set was dictated by other factors. The geopolitics of Eurasia compelled the Manchu rulers to look north and west. Their own northern origins gave precedence to overland concerns; their mission in the south was largely to hold down the people whose loyalty could not be secured. In addition, their feeling of cultural inferiority led them to try to be more Chinese than the Chinese in their ideals of governance, by strengthening the only body of well-tested philosophy known to them, the

Neo-Confucianism of Zhu Xi. It so happened that it was also the most orthodox restatement of Confucian thought there was. It entailed supporting all the strictures that admonished everyone to stay on the land and give filial support to the family by never leaving home, and it looked patronizingly on those who chose the vocation of trade.[18] This determination by the Manchu emperors to be successful in maintaining these strong principles was to have fateful consequences for China during the next two centuries. By the time the Europeans came in force to threaten the China coasts, the Qing court had become totally inflexible regarding these tenets.

What of the Chinese in Southeast Asia when the greatly weakened Ming dynasty was followed by a strong and vigilant new one? The fall of Ming and the loyalist cause which that produced after 1644 may be compared to the exodus of Nationalist supporters from the mainland after 1949. While the political and ideological positions were quite different, the seaward sweep to the coast and the islands, to Taiwan, and then across the seas was similar. In the earlier period, the loyalists went mainly to Vietnam and other parts of Southeast Asia and to Japan, but did not get as far from

China as those after 1949. Fewer of them in the seventeenth century were well educated, and they did not see themselves as emigrating. Albeit but briefly, they did bring a new dimension to the Chinese in Southeast Asia, something beyond trading, a degree of Chinese identity overseas that marked the sojourners, that is, those who resided temporarily away from home.

Many of these sojourners were already outside China in 1644, either with the Zheng Chenggong forces or some other armed band, or simply trading or working in Southeast Asia on their own initiative. Dutch and Spanish writings confirm that there were thousands in their territories, notably in Luzon and Java. Taken together with other sources, these accounts show that thousands more were scattered on the mainland in the Vietnamese and Siamese empires, in native kingdoms and princely states in the Malay Archipelago, notably in Malacca, and in the outlying islands of Moluccas, Makassar, Bali, and West Borneo. They were also to be found in ports on the peripheries of all the major polities, for example, Patani on the Malay Peninsula and the Mekong Delta and the port of Ha-tien, that is, on the marches of what was still Cambodian territory. For most of these Chinese, there was no question of returning to China. But one example of a Chinese overseas community was the one in central Vietnam, the first of the Minh Huong ("Ming incense") villages, which kept alive the flame of loyalty to the Ming dynasty. This implied that the whole community would preserve that loyalty until the opportunity came for them to return to China when the Qing dynasty was overthrown. More typically, however, smaller groups behaved as sojourners and tried to keep together in the port cities. Most married local women, but many arranged for their children and grandchildren to marry within their community in order to retain a Chinese identity as long as possible. From time to time, new male immigrants were available to marry the daughters, and a few sons found their way back their ancestral homes in China to marry and start new families there. How all this was accomplished and what it tells us about the strategies adopted ever since will be examined in Chapter 2.

The sweep by the Chinese from north-central China toward the sea over a period of more than a thousand years was thus always accompanied by the successful transplantation of their earthbound continental values to the whole length of the coast. The indigenous peoples in the south were taught to accept this correct and superior worldview, and they modified their culture and orientation accordingly. In addition, imperial needs demanded that all resources, not least human resources, be drawn upon to ensure that the heartland be defended. In this context, it was established policy that any seaward development deemed not vital for China be curbed. It was enough that foreign countries acknowledged the wealth and power of the empire and were welcomed when they brought tribute. If their traders brought cargoes that China needed, they too would be welcome. It was quite unnecessary for Chinese people themselves to seek out these foreigners and expose the empire to any kind of risk.

As a result a one-sided, and on the whole passive, view of Southeast Asia prevailed along the China coasts. No power in the region was a threat, no indigenous economy was rich enough to stimulate large-scale trade, and no resources there, except possibly rice from Thailand from the eighteenth century, were considered essential to China. Furthermore, apart from the Buddhism imported from India into the region, and that only for about four centuries in the first millennium, no Southeast Asian culture attracted Chinese attention. The conclusion was, therefore, that there was no reason to modify the fundamental premises of a land-bound society dependent on maintaining an effective continental strategy. Given that reality, the coastal people of Guangdong, Fujian, and Zhejiang would have to contain their enterprise and adventurous spirit in the interest of the empire as a whole. Surprising numbers of them did venture forth despite the official bans, but certainly not as many as if the imperial court had supported them the way Western governments had done for their company traders.

The contrast with the free-ranging maritime enterprise of the Europeans is obvious. Suffice it to say that, when Westerners arrived off the coast of China in the 1520s, they were the new actors who provided the impetus for change. Without knowing for another three hundred years what they were doing to China, it was they who started the process that would eventually turn the heads of the Chinese away from the continent to look out toward the sea.

CHAPTER TWO

The Sojourners' Way

For the past half-century, there has been an ongoing debate concerning the nature of Chinese migrants overseas. It hinges on a major disagreement about whether Chinese are like all other migrants when they leave their country, or whether they are quite different. The difference lies in the greater difficulty they seem to have in assimilating in the countries where they settle. This debate has interesting social and cultural facets, but the keenest interest has been in the political ramifications of having unassimilated migrants within modern nation-states. At that level, the issues are so emotive and controversial that it is hardly surprising that there are no widely accepted conclusions about migrants in general and about the Chinese as migrants in particular. But one thing is clear. Assimilated or not, the Chinese overseas did change. They have been variously adaptable, and they have demonstrated that the idea "once a Chinese, always a Chinese" is simply not true. How they did so through their own singular conditions of history, culture, and the force of events peculiar to them, will be the main theme of this chapter.

The concept of assimilation has been difficult to define. Although it is theoretically possible to take any group of migrants and count the individuals among them who observers would agree should be considered assimilated, as compared with those who are clearly not, this approach tells us little about the social dynamics of the group when it acts as a community. It also fails to take into account the history and traditions that guide that community's actions. Many more studies will be needed before the debate can be resolved. And if the issue of assimilation continues to be politicized, such a resolution seems most unlikely. That future prospect, however, need not concern us. What is valuable about the debate is that it has made us more sensitive to the long-term perspective, and has forced the protagonists to go back to historical sources.

Much more pertinent to my theme are definitions for the words *migration* and *migrant*. In modern times, they conjure up two images above all, that of labor recruitment on a large scale following the industrial revolution, and that of immigration requirements and controls established by various governments. The first had been linked, before the rise of the nation-state, to settlement and ultimately assimilation. But since governments have been strictly implementing contracts that enable them to send workers home at the end of their term of labor, labor migration no longer raises questions of assimilation.

The second, however, does. In setting criteria for immigration policy, nation-states are increasingly aware that the admission of those they consider to be suitable immigrants is politically sensitive. The long list of immigration policy reviews in countries like the United States, Australia, and Canada since the nineteenth century and, more recently, in Western Europe, Latin America, Japan, and most of the new nation-states of Asia, testify to the shifting standards that these countries have experienced. Whether the potential immigrant can be assimilated or not has often been the most important issue for policymakers. And the sharper the definition of who might become migrants, the more difficult it is for Chinese migrants to deal with their tradition of sojourning, which others see as a barrier to assimilation. It has become important that the sojourner's way be better understood as modern migration patterns become global.[1]

The concept of sojourning is found in the four major languages of East Asia—Chinese, Korean, Japanese, and Vietnamese. Meaning temporary residence at a new place of abode (with the intention of returning), it originated in China, and may be described as a concept that has evolved through the Chinese experience of migration. The set of norms the Chinese applied to explain and understand the idea of sojourning was based on premises that derived from conditions within China. When used in modern times to examine the phenomenon of emigration and describe what Chinese outside China do, these norms differ considerably from those applied in modern nation-states. It is not only a question of terminology. The very idea of immigration and emigration was not an issue that concerned the Chinese in the past. Foreigners resided in China temporarily throughout history. If they stayed long enough and settled down, they and their communities eventually became Chinese. The few Chinese who sojourned abroad in early times were expected to behave in similar ways, but so few had done so before modern times that little attention was paid to the subject.

Chinese governments down to the end of the nineteenth century even denied that there had been any emigration at all. When the Qing court did note that various kinds of Chinese had been going out of China in small numbers since the tenth century, in larger numbers since the late sixteenth century, and in a veritable flood well beyond the region since the nineteenth, it had to consider how to explain and deal with the phenomenon. Because of the many constraints on the mobility of women and children, most of these emigrants were men. Up to that time, most of the terms used for these men stressed that they were either vagabonds, fugitives, and outlaws, or they were mere sojourners, guests, visitors, only temporarily resident abroad. Thus the official records said little about them. In any case, from the 1370s till 1893, the main thrust of imperial law on the subject of Chinese leaving their country's shores was very clear. If they had no approved reason for being outside the country, these Chinese would be punished as criminals on their return.

The Qing court at the end of the nineteenth century finally became aware that living abroad was not treachery and not a crime, and that those Chinese who were successful elsewhere could actually be an asset to the empire. The mandarins tended to focus on the wealth and expertise of the Chinese abroad to make their case for a change of policy toward such people. They did so without rejecting the orthodox Confucian perspective of any form of emigration. That perspective, which applied to the long periods covered in Chapter 1, looked at what had happened over the centuries in the following way. Throughout the centuries since the Song dynasty (since the tenth century), the Chinese who went overseas in the ports across the South China Sea were not supposed to have left China permanently. If they were good sons who were filial and loved their homes, they would always have planned to return. Thus when they were away from China, they would not have stopped being Chinese. Most of them, if they had sojourned all their lives, and raised a family locally and failed to return home to die, would have tried, wherever possible, to ensure that their children would still consider themselves Chinese.

This normative approach clearly represented a view from the top, an elitist view describing an ideal type. There was ample evidence throughout those centuries that it was not always practicable, and often not true. Chinese writings themselves mention cases of isolated individuals, inevitably male, who had assimilated locally because they were without family or communal support. Others record that many who had acquired wealth and power had done well by being upwardly mobile in the native hierarchies. This had often meant that they married local women, consciously abandoned their Chinese loyalties, and identified totally with the interests of the port cities or kingdoms they chose to live in. These departures from what were expected of good Chinese were not surprising, but no less regrettable in the eyes of their elders in China.

The mandarins, after the Qing empire had joined the "family of nations" in the 1860s, began to argue that the time had come to take note of the coolie labor that was being recruited to work in distant places under appalling conditions. It was time to show concern for the fates of Chinese under foreign jurisdictions. In particular, when it was discovered that identifiably Chinese communities had survived two or more centuries living abroad, especially in Java and other parts of the

Malay Archipelago, the mandarins realized that there should be official recognition for such heroic communities. Those in the upper echelons had become aware, through treaties signed with Western powers, how much attention the Europeans gave to protecting their own citizens overseas. In preparing for imperial representation abroad, including consular offices, the mandarins recommended that the Chinese abroad should be given a respectable place in the Chinese scheme of things. This was eloquently argued by more and more officials during the 1880s. In 1893, the ban on foreign travel was finally lifted.[2] Everyone knew how ineffective the prohibitions had been since the eighteenth century, how often they had been modified and reinterpreted, what hypocrisies were practiced after the two Anglo-Chinese wars in the nineteenth century to pretend that the prohibitions were still law, and how impossible it was to implement such laws among the southern coastal Chinese.

The end of the ban was, of course, primarily a removal of a defunct symbol. What it did not do was to change the underlying assumptions and redefine the overseas Chinese as modern emigrants instead of the sojourners that they had always been. On the contrary, the lifting of the ban was celebrated by a popular call to recognize such Chinese abroad for their past and present contributions, to give them a higher status in official eyes, to encourage them to identify not only with their homes in the coastal provinces but also with China and Chinese civilization. To express all this, a generic title for them was needed. On the one hand, it would replace all the unflattering names they had been called for centuries. On the other, it could invoke a uniform sense of identity among people who had been distinguished from one another by their province or county of origin, or as merchants *(huashang)*, workers and artisans *(huagong)*, and coolies *(kuli)*. Such a title should also convey approval, and capture the spirit of what Chinese culture expected from good Chinese.

Thus was evolved the new term for these Chinese, the *huaqiao*, the Chinese sojourner.[3] The idea of *qiao* (temporarily located) had an ancient and distinguished pedigree. The word had been used for several centuries during a major division of China between north and south, the Northern and Southern dynasties of the fourth to sixth centuries. It was used to give official recognition to elite families from the north who were forced by foreign invasion to abandon their homes and follow the Jin dynasty south to Nanjing and elsewhere south of the Yangzi River. Thereafter it remained an elegant term occurring in poetry and essays, reflecting the fact that officials and literati were often required to be away from their ancestral homes for indefinite periods. It was never used to depict the usual reasons for leaving home, such as to make a living, to trade, to seek one's fortune, or to migrate in search for a better place to settle. Instead, it captured a sense of doing what had to be done, fulfilling a duty, and emphasized noble and dignified actions that benefited others as well as oneself.

As outlined in Chapter 1, these sentiments originated in an earthbound agrarian society. In the terms acceptable to such a society, migrations in history, represented by words like *yimin* (moved people), *liumin* (dispersed people), or *nanmin* (refugees) and others, had followed established patterns, including

1. The official moving of people to border areas to defend the frontiers, or of those from areas of crop failure to places where food was plentiful, or where new lands were available for cultivation.
2. The movement of refugees from war, floods, famine, or other natural disasters.

3. The flight of exiles for a host of reasons, including rebels, criminals, and other fugitives from the law.

Not included in these patterns were the movements of officials sent out as part of their duties, students studying away from home, and merchants seeking markets for their goods and traveling to transport them. They were all merely sojourning, with every intention of returning home.

For the first millennium A.D., none of the three common migration patterns just mentioned led the Chinese to move overseas. There was ample space for all three within China, and migrations filled the more sparsely populated areas, the uplands, and the marshy delta districts on the coasts. The few officials sent out on missions and the students of Buddhism who set out for holy places in India mostly returned when their tasks were done. Similarly, merchants who traded overseas would have made regular journeys (in Southeast Asia, probably one return trip each year following the monsoons) and rarely stayed away longer than necessary. We must assume that their numbers were negligible. There was nothing experienced during this period that would challenge the core of agrarian values that normally kept everyone at home.

Indeed, the push for the Chinese to cross the South China Sea and stay out for long periods, if not actually abandon hopes of returning, began only following disasters that befell the imperial order. No significant reference to sojourning communities overseas appeared until after the fall of the Southern Song dynasty to the Mongols at the end of the thirteenth century. For the first time, all of China was conquered by a foreign power and many refugees, rebels or loyalists, and certain categories of traders left the China coasts to find new homes in the region. At least three groups can be observed, one in Annan (now northern Vietnam), another in Champa (now central Vietnam) and the other in Zhenla (Cambodia). A century later, other traders and sailors were left abroad after the fall of the Mongol Yuan in 1368, notably those who went to Java and Sumatra. This second exodus was in part due to the ban on private foreign trade that had been introduced by the first Ming emperor. Some of the sojourners had married local women, raised families, and formed small communities at various ports, but the ban ensured that their numbers were not augmented. As a result, the majority of them would have assimilated, leaving little trace of organized Chinese group activity in the region when the Europeans first arrived at the beginning of the sixteenth century. Individual sojourners had disappeared, underlining a fundamental principle of sojourning. Sojourning depends on regular contact with the home country, or at least frequent access to things from home. It cannot survive if the sojourners see no prospect of returning home at all.

What saved the Chinese phenomenon was the expansion of foreign trading activity, with more Southeast Asians, Japanese, and Europeans seeking trade on the China coasts, and the relaxing after 1567 of the Ming dynasty's official ban on private foreign trade. By the seventeenth century, small sojourning communities had been established in every major Southeast Asian port. Their numbers were greatly augmented when the Manchu armies conquered South China and forced many of those who were still loyal to the Ming imperial house to stay in the region. This was true especially of the followers of Zheng Chenggong (or Koxinga) after the end of their regime in Taiwan in 1683. Thereafter, the effectiveness of these sojourners as distinct Chinese communities depended on the local authorities in the region. If the outsiders were useful to their hosts as Chinese, especially in the way they served the China trade, they enjoyed privileges and even monopolies. If they were seen as potential threats, especially when European powers like the Spanish and the Dutch felt outnumbered and insecure, they were massacred or driven out. Under no circumstances could these Chinese turn to the imperial court for help.

It had taken the mandarin class a long time to appreciate the achievements of the overseas Chinese. The earthbound mind-set that denied them legitimacy did not crack even when reports of Western maritime domination in the region were reaching the Qing court. Provincial officials in Fujian and Guangdong had noted throughout the eighteenth century the range of activities that various dialect groups in their provinces (the Hokkien, Teochiu, Cantonese, Hakka, and Hainanese) were engaged in. Some of the books written during this period mention the activities of such Chinese, including the major seventeenth-century book by Zhang Xie, *Dong xiyang kao* (Studies of the eastern and western oceans),[4] and the equally informative eighteenth-century work by Chen Lunjiong, the *Haiguo wenjianlu* (A record of things heard and seen of the maritime countries).⁵ Others were by Wang Dahai, the *Haidao yizhi* (An informal record of the islands)⁶ and by Xie Qinggao, the *Hai lu* (An account of the seas).⁷ Xie Qinggao did his traveling in the late eighteenth century, though his notes were written down early in the nineteenth. These works show that more and more Chinese were progressively involved in Southeast Asian trade, often in tandem with, and under the aegis and protection of, either local rulers or European trading organizations. These writings attested to the prominence of many Chinese sojourning communities, in Faifo (now Hoi An, central Vietnam), in Ayutthaya and then in Bangkok, in Patani and the isthmus of the Malay Peninsula, in Manila and other islands of the Spanish Philippines, and in Batavia, Malacca, and Dutch-controlled parts of the Malay Archipelago. Yet it was not until after several decisive defeats by the European powers of the Chinese empire in the second half of the nineteenth century that a name for these Chinese and their misfortunes and achievements was found.

Traditional sojourning had become a condition of the China trade. It survived because governments in the region encouraged it. But it was also a state of mind, a residual affirmation of the sojourner's ultimate identification with China. That sojourning was finally recognized as beneficial, as another kind of loyalty to things Chinese, was a belated development. This recognition was greatly welcome among those who had been practicing it unheard and unseen, and without having a name to describe what they were doing. What crystallized the recognition of the phenomenon was the challenge to national consciousness, the call for a new patriotism to help an enfeebled China to defend itself against the aggressive West. The introduction of the term *huaqiao*, the term that encapsulated the experience of sojourning, did not create that phenomenon. But by giving the phenomenon an elegant and respectable name, it gave sojourning a definite direction and a new purposefulness, and made it into a powerful political force in the twentieth century.

The objective fact of sojourning can be said to represent the Chinese approach to experimental migration. The subjective belief in sojourning, however, delineated the extent to which the Chinese clung to their connections with China. How did the official approval given to sojourning affect what the Chinese overseas actually did? A comparison of the sojourner's way before and after 1900, the old sojourning with the new sojourning, reveals important differences that are still relevant today.

BEFORE 1900

I have already commented on early forms of the old sojourning tradition of the seventeenth and eighteenth centuries. Studies show that, among the small numbers of Chinese who dealt successfully with indigenous elites, intermarriage and assimilation were common, and isolated individuals undertook both readily. But there was no uniform pattern of response after the Europeans arrived. For example, where the Europeans were in authority, as in the Philippines and in Java, their respective policies were sharply different. The Spanish policy favored assimilation through conversion to Catholicism, and ensured that all indigenous women who married Chinese men remained Catholics and brought up Catholic mestizo families. By the mid-eighteenth century, the Spanish had severely restricted the number of new Chinese permitted in their territory and turned to these assimilated mestizos as the only Chinese they could trust to work with them. In contrast, the Dutch who extended their control over the north coast of Java in the eighteenth century preferred to segregate the Chinese from the indigenous peoples and also from themselves. The policy was established from their start in Batavia at the beginning of the seventeenth century. A virtue was made of having each racial and ethnic group preserve its own way of life, but clearly there were economic and political advantages in using the Chinese to advance the China trade and in preventing alliances between the Chinese and native elites against Dutch rule. The result was that, by the eighteenth century, the Chinese mestizo identified fully with what had begun to achieve political recognition as the Philippines, while the local-born, or *peranakan*, of Batavia and other Javanese cities were free to consolidate their own identifiably Chinese communities. The latter preserved the qualities of sojourners that were eventually to gain formal recognition by China later on.[8]

But, for the majority, sojourning was found in three forms, the first stage when the community was all male, the second when the men who married local wives grouped together to form family communities, and the third when new male arrivals marrying into these communities brought fresh Chinese perspectives and reminded all of them of the sojourning norms. This pattern is not at all like the migratory practices of the Jewish diaspora of a comparable period, nor like the colonists of Western Europe who settled in the Americas and later in Australasia.

The most important form was the first. The sojourners were all adult males, most of whom left their wives and children at home in China. No females were allowed to leave home and the official ban made it impossible for families to travel outside the Chinese empire. The strategies used by males who decided to stay on overseas and form their own community centered on the use of popular religious practices. What emerged as standard practice throughout Southeast Asia was to establish the first (usually Taoist) altar to a common deity that the group preferred; this helped to strengthen social bonds and promote confidence . The next step was to start nonreligious defensive organizations such as triad societies, and then build temples linked to well-known temples of the China coasts. These included Buddhist and other Taoist deities. Eventually, the growing communities evolved larger social organizations that local governments saw fit to recognize. There were minor variations, but the male communities needed this kind of start to launch their enterprises, to support their widening range of activities, and to enable them to recruit reinforcements from their families and home villages, thus producing the phenomenon of chain migration from China. This remained the initial basic practice of the sojourner, and the practice survived well into the nineteenth century. It was only gradually displaced when men could bring their family members to join them early in the twentieth century, after the ban on foreign travel was finally lifted in 1893.

In any case, before 1893 relatively few stayed with these pioneering organizations beyond the first generation. Ultimately most of these males either returned to China or married indigenous women. Those who stayed on and intermarried locally then produced the second form of sojourning, the family community. Classic examples were the *peranakan* or *baba* (local-born) communities of Java and Melaka (Malacca), which emerged as a dominant model in the Malay world during the eighteenth century. These communities were established when the males (many of whom already had wives in China) fathered children and wanted, in particular, their male descendants to retain what they considered to be Chinese virtues essential to their social and commercial well-being. Without the benefit of formal education, this was achieved by the continuation of religious and other customary practices, notably everything pertaining to birth, marriage, and death and the best-known calendrical festivals. Male children, however, were also introduced to basic elements of the Chinese language, particularly the spoken dialect of their fathers, to enable them to sustain the vital links with the growing China trade. And the China trade, especially when it enabled the males to travel to China from time to time, provided them with key ingredients of a more or less Chinese lifestyle, and reinforced the tradition of sojourning. Thus to remain Chinese required frequent contacts with China. Those who had wives and children in China might also bring their Chinese sons out to help, and even ultimately inherit, the overseas business. These sons, who would have learned to read and write Chinese before they came, would also assist with the task of cultural maintenance among the local members of the family.

The third form depended on fresh supplies of males from China, and only occurred in places where the local rulers, whether indigenous or European, allowed them to come continuously. The numbers of such Chinese remained small until the eighteenth century. The new migrants had the vigor and ambition that the older Chinese males wanted for their businesses, and some of them provided husbands for the *peranakan* or mestizo women. They were also living reminders of evolving social and religious practices in China, and could communicate a sense of what was expected of Chinese who had to live overseas. In the process they helped the community resist pressures to assimilate. This supply of *xinke*, or *sinkeh* (newcomers), could not be counted on to be regular and reliable until economic conditions began to deteriorate in southern China and improve markedly in Southeast Asia late in the eighteenth century and the early decades of the nineteenth century. After that, its impact on community formation along increasingly Chinese lines was strong. Subsequent efforts involved ensuring a degree of formal Chinese traditional learning and a heightened pride in being Chinese—a process that has been described as resinicization.

All this was in the context of trading communities whose size was severely limited by official policies both in China and in the region. These policies were relaxed in the nineteenth century with the advent of the industrial revolution and the end of slavery in the Western world. It was no accident that the need for a freer flow of labor to the mines and plantations opened up by the new generation of European capitalists coincided with the series of coastal wars that opened up China for international trade. China's several defeats by foreign powers in the coastal provinces opened the doors for labor emigration, increasingly to territories farther away in the Americas and Australasia. The first rush of coolie workers, replacing slaves for the back-breaking work of opening up frontier lands in various parts of the Americas, was unprotected by any agreement with China.[9] Most of the coolies were abominably treated, but some of the survivors stayed on. In some areas, where intermarriage was possible, examples of assimilation in the next generation could be found, but most Chinese settled down in small mainly male communities, to live the lives of sojourners.

On the surface, the members of these first communities, who lived among largely European migrant societies, organized themselves in ways resembling those that had appeared much earlier in Asia. But in reality there were great differences. To begin with, who were these Chinese who left China in such large numbers during the nineteenth century? Whether in an exodus in search of gold in California or Victoria in Australia, or as contract labor organized for work in industrial teams, there had never been such kinds of Chinese leaving China before. They had no connection with influential people in China or abroad, and most of them did not even have previous trading experience. Never had so many traveled such long distances to places where there had not been earlier Chinese trading communities. Never had there been such a sizable challenge of numbers to authorities who themselves were controlled by recent migrants from Europe, as was the case with Australasia, Canada, and the United States. Never had Chinese labor moved among peoples who saw themselves as economically and technologically superior, or tried to compete with foreign workers with a new and hitherto unrecognized class consciousness. And never before had the Chinese encountered fellow workers, equally disadvantaged and equally untutored, who considered themselves racially and culturally superior as well.[10] One further unique feature was found only in the United States. In the midst of anti-Chinese discrimination, there had come young Chinese students and officials in search of a modern education. Although the group was small in number, never before had a mass of laborers been followed by such esteemed fellow countrymen and, remarkably, a group that was to mark the beginnings of a historic educational movement in the next century.

These circumstances ensured that, except for a few individuals, there was no alternative to sojourning for the Chinese who were left in the Americas and Australasia after the gold rush was over and after contracts came to an end. Because exclusionary policies were introduced that kept women out, very few Chinese families could be settled or created. The Chinatown communities clung on, but most were destined not to survive as the older male members died or returned to China. That the Chinese did not consider themselves migrants like the Europeans was understandable, since they had not intended to remain outside China for long. But it cannot be said that they were consciously sojourning, if only because the phenomenon had not been discerned and the concept was still unidentified. What they were doing had yet to have a name.

Nevertheless, they were in some ways more sojourners than their predecessors in Southeast Asia had ever been in earlier centuries. Despite the greater distances, the range of personal links with their families at home in China was easier. Diplomatic relations with China had been established, and some consular representation was available in several American countries. News of China, even books and newspapers from China, reached the Chinese in the West almost as quickly as they had begun to reach the Chinese in Southeast Asia. Unlike the latter, who had endured long periods of alienation from governments in China that had ignored them and did not care for them, even the poorest of those coolies who left China in the second half of the nineteenth century could sense a sharpening of the sense of Chinese identity, the prelude to the nationalism that was about to burst upon all Chinese.

The way in which the sojourners of this period sought to remain Chinese was thus part of a new beginning. The experiences of their predecessors could remind them how much more difficult it had been to ensure that their descendants would stay Chinese. But if their predecessors could achieve the measure of success that many of them did, the objective conditions by 1900, with a China more aware of and concerned for their fate, could be described as being much more favorable. The fact that, by this time, sojourners were welcome in the colonial and semi-colonial territories of Southeast Asia while those in the European migrant states were systematically ejected was a cruel difference that only heightened the desire to elevate the issue of overseas Chinese to a level never dreamed of even a few years before.

AFTER 1900

By the end of the nineteenth century, the tradition of sojourning had been given a new name, that of *qiao*. The sojourners, now called *huaqiao*, were legitimized. Thus began the new sojourning, which left the realm of stealth and secrecy, of outcasts and adventurers, and of low-class coolie backgrounds. In its place, for the next half-century, was the image of endurance, enterprise, and courage, mixed up with China's vague concern that the Chinese identity of these new sojourners was of rather poor quality and needed to be helped to reach higher standards. Also growing was the realization that the sojourners had been forsaken for too long, that foreign powers had exploited their talents to enrich their countries, that many were already lost to "barbarian" ways. A developing sense of urgency called for these national assets to be suitably endorsed and the energies of the *huaqiao* channeled to serve China.

The transformation of the China coast following the opening of the treaty ports had forced the Qing government to redefine its relationship with its Chinese subjects. In particular, the reports of diplomatic officials like Xue Fucheng and Huang Zunxian, and the essays by men in the world of business like Zheng Guanying in cities like Hong Kong and Shanghai, had prepared the Chinese for an awakening to a world of foreign travel and residence, even settlement.[11] The bizarre kidnapping of Sun Yat-sen in London in 1896 highlighted the fact that he had traveled among his compatriots overseas and that his fellow Cantonese outside China had responded warmly to his appeals to overthrow the Qing government.[12] The advocacy of radical reforms by literati like Kang Youwei and Liang Qichao after China's defeat by Japan in 1895 raised expectations for a few months in 1898. But what was truly significant was the reception that Kang and Liang, as the first famous literati who were not holding any office, were given when they traveled as exiles among the Chinese overseas.[13] Suddenly the large numbers of

Chinese scattered around Southeast Asia, and even the small groups in the West, themselves attracted national attention as none had ever done before.

The results were dramatic. The discovery that there were sojourners who were open to new ideas, who were skilled in dealing with native and European governments, and whose overseas experience might be called upon to play a role in China's affairs, galvanized the Qing government and its critics and opponents alike. At one level, news and commentary about the overseas Chinese expanded manifold. Scholars and officials reached for the historical texts that mentioned these people, especially the anecdotes of those spectacularly successful in Southeast Asia since the Song dynasty. At another level, both the Qing government and the reformist and revolutionary organizations wooed the *huaqiao* especially for their financial support, the former for the empire's economic development and the latter for the reform of the Qing dynasty or the overthrow of the Manchu.

Much of the competition for support during the first decade of this century is now well documented, and the details need not detain us. The *huaqiao* response was warm, if not uniformly enthusiastic. Their willingness to bring investments and technical knowledge back to China was both understandable and hardly surprising. What was less expected of the overseas Chinese was the willing support given to Sun Yat-sen's nationalism, the easy identification with the rebel traditions that permeated Chinese society, and the speed of politicization among the poor and illiterate, or barely literate, among them. Perhaps the following crude verses written about 1903 and addressed to the less responsive rich sojourners in Southeast Asia sum up the political message best. They come from the highly emotional *Song of Revolution* (Geming ge), which was widely circulated and is thought to have been very influential at the time.[14]

Let me call again to the *huaqiao* overseas,
Compatriots to the distant ends of the earth!
. . . . . .
The pestilential Nanyang air fills the skies.
Life is short when the deadly fevers come.

The theme of dying abroad, and their wealth not being able to save them, runs through the whole poem. It goes on to ask,

What use is the cumulation of silver cash?
Why not use it to eject the Manchus?

The poem then suggests that a hundred thousand quick-loading rifles should get rid of the Manchus and, with a republican polity established, the *huaqiao* could vent their feelings against the Europeans who have treated the Chinese overseas with contempt. Then follows the most serious admonition,

It is hard to be happy all one's life,
You need but little conscience to feel shame.
What then is the most shameful matter?
To forget one's ancestors deserves the greatest hate!
If not that, then to register as a foreign national
Forgetting that you come from Chinese stock.

The verses marked a decisive shift in tone: for China to care for the *huaqiao*, they must bear a corresponding responsibility and pay a price, not only in cash and patriotic support, but also in a recommitment to traditional values, the core of the sojourning ethic.

The fall of the Qing and the establishment of the Republic of China in 1911 confirmed the new era for sojourners. Calling them *huaqiao* was not merely finding them a new name. The appellation involved a normative exercise that affirmed a national consciousness, a faith in the rejuvenation of China, and a name to be worn as a badge of pride. Sojourning became a national duty, with the republican government responsible for the sojourners' preservation and protection. An Overseas Chinese Affairs Department eventually emerged under the Ministry of Foreign Affairs. Its work, expanding beyond fund-raising and diplomatic protection, was also to cover education and identity retention. Programs for new textbooks and training teachers from China to teach among the *huaqiao* left an enduring heritage that not only supported sojourning but confirmed it as a patriotic obligation.

Sun Yat-sen and his followers kept faith with the *huaqiao* around the world who had helped them at the time of their greatest need. When the Guomindang came to power in 1928, the commitment to promote overseas Chinese welfare became even stronger. The image of the patriotic *huaqiao* was supplemented by official determination to keep all sojourners patriotic. This was accomplished not only through consular offices but also through locally recruited Guomindang party members who regularly received honors from the Nanjing government. Scholars in China were encouraged to study the overseas Chinese in greater depth. A new research center at Jinan University, then in Shanghai, was established, and books, monographs, journals, and magazines were published to deal with the mountains of data being collected about overseas Chinese.[15] Attention was given to the fact that foreign and colonial governments were systematically reporting on these sojourners. Particularly impressive were the volumes published by the Japanese on the business activities conducted by the Chinese in Southeast Asia, some of which were immediately translated into Chinese, not to mention the many more secret reports that were not published.[16]

Chinese government efforts had differing results in the two major groups of *huaqiao*, those in Southeast Asia and those in the migrant states of the Americas and Australasia. The government's policies had less impact in the migrant states because they coincided with a period when the sojourners there were aging and much reduced in numbers, and no fresh immigration was allowed. Nevertheless, the sojourner communities in North America and Australia were greatly inspired by the attention they received. Although unsuccessful in lifting their status in these migrant states, the efforts by the Chinese government were appreciated and the Chinese there remained patriotic and involved. For those in the United States, the presence of large numbers of Chinese students in colleges and universities added a lofty dimension to the lives of the sojourners themselves.

In Southeast Asia, increasing wealth brought more sojourners, including large numbers of teachers, journalists, and other professionals who were more prone to come and go. Warlordism, endemic banditry, civil war, and economic disruptions in South China also kept the supply of Chinese labor in Southeast Asia up. And since most patriotic *huaqiao* already abroad preferred to stay outside China, ever greater efforts were made by the Chinese government to harness their patriotism to help a divided and impoverished China. Colonial governments, in response, were increasingly alarmed by the rising Chinese nationalism, and took steps to counter China's control over the behavior of local Chinese. They did so by allowing whole families to immigrate and inducing them to settle down, and also by building more colonial schools to encourage the young to cultivate local loyalties. The tensions between various groups of the Chinese themselves began to grow, notably between those who had learned Chinese and looked to China and those who were educated in local or colonial languages. At the same time, sojourner nationalism aroused fears among emerging indigenous nationalist leaders, forcing them to pay close attention to Chinese ambitions and promote their own nationalism against that of the Chinese.

The height of Chinese nationalism was reached in and outside China during the Sino-Japanese war and World War II. *Huaqiao* were deeply concerned about the dangers to China, and many devoted themselves to the national cause. But more interesting was the intense interaction of traditional and modern ideas outside the framework of China, an interaction that kept conditions fluid and even threatened the Chinese overseas with something of a paradox. Traditional values had first inhibited the Chinese from leaving home. The newly reinterpreted idea of sojourning early in this century then justified their staying overseas while asking that they remain loyal to their Chinese identity. But modern nationalism increasingly demanded new commitments, which should logically have led the patriotic sojourners to return to China to help China's development or to fight to save the country from foreign conquest. If the *huaqiao* followed that logic, it would paradoxically have greatly diminished their own ranks as sojourners. But, in fact, they stayed out in ever increasing numbers, because they knew they had a better life outside China.

For the true sojourner, the pull of China was beyond intellectual curiosity. Many Chinese families in Southeast Asia carefully prepared their young to look northward, and Chinese schools were immensely popular. Many went to study in universities in China after graduating from high school. Studying Chinese and knowing China became for some the underlying meaning of life itself. The Chinese language was seen as the key. Snippets of poetry and literary prose to be learned by rote and the mental wrestling with selected classical texts were vital to literacy. But the education laid down by officials in Nanjing and the textbooks published in Shanghai were nothing if not modern. Over and above the study of traditional values and Chinese history, the emphasis was increasingly on science and mathematics as the skills that China most desperately needed. For *huaqiao* to be patriotic, they were most encouraged to learn all that was new from outside China so that they could return one day to become truly useful to their country.[17] But China itself was changing, and many sojourners were bewildered and torn between various kinds of loyalties. They had to look in many directions at the same time, including the need to adapt to the local modernizing environments in which they had grown up and hoped to go on living. They had also to search for new ways of earning a living, if not to make their fortunes.

The sojourner communities in various parts of Southeast Asia were not at all homogeneous. Economic and technological changes in some parts of the region enabled different groups of sojourners to know much more of the outside world. Their interactions with many varieties of indigenous Southeast Asians, different kinds of Europeans and Eurasians, with other Asian migrants and sojourners such as the Indians, the Japanese, the Jews, and various kinds of Muslims, enlarged their range of experience. The younger local-born Chinese included many who did not wish to return to China. Many could not speak or read Chinese, but had received their education in European languages. They had gone to many different types of schools, receiving an education that was enriching and broadening and did not necessarily endorse any single tradition. The miscellanies of modern ideas and practices the local-born encountered in the multicultural societies they grew up in often challenged the idea that there was only one kind of patriotic Chinese. Individuals sought, and sometimes found, their own cultural amalgam in which they could lodge a Chinese ethnic loyalty—but for many of them, neither tradition nor modernity alone could explain the complex and changing world in which they found themselves.

Sojourning evolved among traditional Chinese at a time when the empire did not welcome them home; it evolved as a strategy for remaining abroad while awaiting a chance to return. The modern idea of *huaqiao* was a new norm for encouraging political loyalty from sojourners. It was accompanied by offers of official protection in return. This latter political concept was a product of modern nationalism, and it was effective as long it was taken in isolation. But when it encountered other people's nationalism, it could be the source of conflict and much anguish for the *huaqiao* themselves. And when the numbers of such patriotic sojourners were large, as they were in Southeast Asia, the time came when the very idea of sojourning had to give way. That time came soon after the end of World War II. The sojourner's way had led to an impasse, to a narrowing of options. Most of the patriotic *huaqiao* had no alternative but to return to China. The less patriotic and the skeptical were given the choice of assimilating into other loyalties, or finding new means to be themselves in increasingly multicultural societies. By the 1950s, for a host of reasons, the sojourning Chinese were poised once again for change.

CHAPTER THREE

The Multicultural Quest for Autonomy

The premodern phenomenon of Chinese sojourning was made respectable at the end of the nineteenth century and became highly politicized during the first half of the twentieth. The interventionist policies of the Republic of China (1912–1949) led to continuous calls for patriotism and financial support that were brought to every overseas Chinese community. These were often generalized exhortations applicable to all Chinese and were used to address the *huaqiao* in any part of the world. But not all sojourners, especially the local-born, cared to respond politically to Chinese nationalism. While proud of being Chinese, these small groups were not necessarily attracted to the new Chinese national identity.

Government and party officials in China assumed that all sojourners were equally willing to identify with whatever cause was dominant in China. They ignored the less visible and deliberately low-key and nonpolitical groups that did not want to make a display of their Chinese heritage. These groups were either sensitive to local conditions or simply uncomfortable with Chinese nationalism. The calls for loyalty to China did not take into account the very different conditions under which the various sojourner communities lived. Patriotism and China's salvation were seen as absolute concepts and, unless they were drummed into the sojourners who were living far away from home, it was feared that the message would not be heard. Such tactics were very damaging for the Chinese overseas, who were seen as potentially disloyal subjects in the countries in which they lived. It would take decades of effort to dispel the picture of every Chinese as someone always loyal to China and never fully attached to his or her adopted home.[1]

Earlier I described sojourning communities that retained a sense of their Chinese identity, some of them for centuries. These were the families or small communities in Southeast Asia who were well settled and had been willing to adopt local customs, or adapt their Chinese practices in ways that would not offend local society. They were respected for their distinctive ethnicity, and were often the only Chinese with whom native elites and Europeans would communicate. They could be found all over the region, some remaining more Chinese for longer periods than others. In some territories, many would eventually assimilate into local elite societies, either through intermarriage or by seeking high public office and thus raising the status of their families.[2]

But where political, demographic, cultural, and economic circumstances made assimilation undesirable or very difficult, as in parts of the Netherlands East Indies and the British empire in Southeast Asia where the dominant populations were Muslim, new kinds of local-born Chinese communities emerged. Those among them who were active in business worked hard at engaging teachers and establishing schools to ensure that their male descendants were Chinese enough to inherit and conduct their China-dependent businesses. They had little access to the classical education associated with the highest standards of Chineseness, but much of that was irrelevant in any case to their immediate need to survive within sojourning communities. Instead, they had come to recognize that, unlike in China, wealth was the most important factor in securing their community's autonomy. They also realized that sensitivity in cross-cultural relations, especially in dealing with European officials and traders and with native aristocrats, was invaluable for their community's prosperity. In addition, their ability to live in multicultural societies would make them locally acceptable at all levels.

In Chapter 2, I focused on the way in which these traditional sojourners, who did not have a name for what they were doing, were given formal recognition as patriotic *huaqiao* at the beginning of the twentieth century. That patriotism reached its climax in the 1940s when the effort to support the anti-Japanese war in China was at its height and was ultimately rewarded by China's attainment of great power status in the United Nations. This patriotic model, however, became double-edged when China became communist and former colonies in Southeast Asia became nation-states. After 1949, especially in the anticommunist nation-states, every Chinese was suspected of being a communist, or at least a sympathizer, whose loyalty could never be trusted. This problem was compounded by the fact that China appealed to patriotic *huaqiao* to return to help build socialism. Among those who considered themselves patriots, most returned. But the majority, who did not share such intense patriotism—especially the local-born—remained behind. They were made aware of the several alternatives of assimilation, integration, and acculturation, words that came to be increasingly used by local political and community leaders. These were concepts found in the social science literature of the day, and much of their respectability derived from the model of the successful "melting pot" in the United States.

If one option was assimilation, the other was found in the experience of traditional sojourners, that is, the settled but unassimilated Chinese in the past whose strategies had enabled their communities to survive for generations. These included those of Chinese descent who had intermarried freely with Vietnamese, Thais, Burmese, and Cambodians on the Southeast Asian mainland. Also included were the Chinese mestizos from the many different islands of the Philippines, who still worked closely with newly arrived Chinese. But most distinctive of all were the *peranakan*, literally the local-born (also known as *baba* or Straits Chinese), of the Dutch and British territories of the Malay Archipelago.[3]

Through the first half of the twentieth century, the local-born survived China's patriotic pressures. They sought their cultural autonomy by subtly and unobtrusively resisting both local assimilation and the efforts by Chinese officials and newly arrived sojourners to resinicize them. But there were other factors. Their story of cultural maintenance was something new among the Chinese overseas, and it helps us understand the modern diaspora of the second half of the twentieth century.[4] Five aspects of that story will be examined here.

TARGETS FOR RESINICIZATION

The first aspect concerns the local-born as *targets for resinicization*. The local-born had been variously acculturated after living for generations outside China, and many of them were considered by newcomers from China to be less than Chinese. They were, therefore, under great pressure to meet the standards set down for patriotic *huaqiao*. The standards were incorporated in school textbooks distributed around the world, and were enunciated repeatedly through strong exhortatory writings that spelled out how true Chinese ought to behave. In exclusively Chinese schools, and among recent immigrants who were primarily Chinese-educated, the standards could be upheld. But most of the local-born found these standards far too demanding. Many of them spoke little or no Chinese, preferred local food (and typically developed their own distinctive cuisine), could speak the local languages fluently, and often identified with the ruling colonial powers.

The Japanese occupation of most of Southeast Asia in 1941–1945, however, highlighted the commonality of those who were locally born with their compatriots in China. Under conditions of war and deprivation, differences between the local-born and the China-born ceased to matter. They were all Chinese and all subject to the same treatment, not only in the eyes of the Japanese enemy but also increasingly in the eyes of the local nationalists, whom the Japanese appeared to encourage. It is thus ironic that the Japanese were responsible for the resinicization of the local-born to a much greater degree than were the exhortations of the Chinese government. Had the allied forces not won the war, no doubt the resinicization process among the local-born would have gone much deeper.[5]

As it was, China was counted among the victors, and all Chinese in Asia and in the migrant states felt both relief and pride. Most of them were willing to identify with the new world order in which China would have a superior place. In North America, the patriotic *huaqiao* had renewed hope of improving their position as sojourners. But the civil war in China was resumed, and the Nanjing government, which had been so close to these *huaqiao* for decades, lost that war and retreated to Taiwan. The competition between the communists and the nationalists for the hearts and minds of the *huaqiao* continued, but the underlying issue was less resinicization than support for the political legitimacy of the government in Taiwan, or conformity with the revolutionary nationalism on the mainland.

The cold war emphasis on ideology after 1949 permeated all Chinese communities overseas. To resinicize was therefore seen by many to mean siding with the communists. But if the Chinese overseas wanted to resist communist ideology, they now had greater options whether they were local-born or not. Many were eligible for local citizenship in their countries of residence, and they finally began to think of settling permanently outside China and acquiring a new nationality. If they still wished to, some could look to the defeated regime on Taiwan, or revert to traditional sojourner behavior and try to preserve as much of their Chinese identity as they could. Many in Southeast Asia chose to move closer to the indigenous forces who replaced colonial rule with newly legitimate national regimes. In the European migrant states in the Americas and Australasia, however, the Chinese had to find new ways of gaining political and social acceptance. These ways, conforming to the standards of the dominant white majorities, included intense concentration on education for the professions and cautious and gradual involvement in social and political affairs. Those who were not able to pursue one of the professions faced certain limitations, but almost all could take advantage of the prospects for upward economic mobility.

By the late 1950s, as the Guomindang government's claim to rule over all of China lost credibility and local nationalisms in Southeast Asia became demanding, the options for the local-born were reduced to starker alternatives. They could choose to move toward gradual cultural integration and assimilation, or they could embark on a new struggle for preservation as members of distinct ethnic groups. Either way, the local-born were freed from the pressures of resinicization for the first time since the beginning of the century. The task of seeking and maintaining an identity was not unfamiliar to them. Their fathers and earlier ancestors, the founders of *peranakan* or *baba* communities, had had to devise strategies for doing just that as traditional sojourners. But in a world of nation-states that was increasingly interdependent, the old strategies would need to be updated if not changed altogether.

SHARING ELITE STATUS

The second part of our story I have called *sharing elite status*. This process was in sharp contrast to the first, and referred to the fact that the local-born had also been the targets of localization, that is, they had been wooed, by colonial and native officials and leaders alike, to join them as local elites and help rule over other Chinese who had arrived more recently. After World War II ended in Southeast Asia, when the colonial governments briefly returned, there was an official reaching out toward Chinese who wanted to settle and not return to China. This approach was continued by some of the national governments that took over when the colonial officials departed. Where they could, these governments, whether in the Philippines, Vietnam, or Burma, also offered public positions to those among their nationals of Chinese descent whose loyalty could be counted on. In such cases, the individuals'

Chinese origins were discounted as long as they no longer identified with either Beijing or Taipei. These practices provided an example for other Chinese, and affirmed the policy that such Chinese were welcome to stay if they were prepared to localize themselves.

For those who had identified fully with Thai nationalism, their access to elite positions was particularly remarkable. Many were leaders in academia and the professions, others served as cabinet ministers, and a few were chosen or elected to become prime minister of Thailand.

In Indonesia, during the early years of independence, some Chinese were allowed to share elite status and help rule their Chinese compatriots. From the late 1950s, however, and especially during the thirty-two years of Suharto's presidency, which ended in May 1998, Chinese participation was increasingly confined to specific areas of trade and investment. Contrary to expectation, this did not ensure greater acceptance by the indigenous population. Indeed, their economic success made them increasingly the targets of violent populist attacks. When the Suharto regime failed to weather the financial crisis in 1997–98, these attacks became increasingly severe and totally damaged the confidence of the Chinese in their future. The uncertainty these Chinese face will make it difficult for them to contribute willingly and effectively to the economic recovery the country needs. And this in turn will not endear them to Indonesia's growing numbers of the indigenous poor and disadvantaged.[6]

In British Malaya (this included Singapore), where Chinese numbers were exceptionally large, it was understood that the Chinese would be given an important place after independence. They were encouraged to participate in local politics and prove their loyalty by helping to fight off the challenge of the Malayan Communist Party. If successful, the party, whose members were predominantly Chinese, would have threatened not only all non-Chinese interests but also the Chinese business elites and the local-born Chinese who feared its identification with Chinese nationalism in a more radicalized form.

Participation in local national politics led to a greater Chinese commitment to their host countries than most leaders expected. The opportunity to participate led many to demonstrate their loyalty openly, join the leading political parties and even organizing new ones.

There is no doubt that the sharing of elite status contributed directly to settlement, loyalty, and the ending of the sojourner outlook for most Chinese Malaysians or Singaporeans. The tolerant leadership of Tengku Abdul Rahman, the first prime minister of the Federation of Malaya and the father of Malaysia, was particularly successful in winning the confidence of the Chinese. And when Singapore became independent in 1965 under Prime Minister Lee Kuan Yew's People's Action Party, the enthusiastic participation of local Chinese in the political process demolished the old idea that overseas Chinese were apolitical. When it really mattered, the ethnic Chinese were ready to be fully involved in loyal citizenship and the task of nation building.[7]

The idea that local-born Chinese could gain sufficient acceptance to join the ruling elites did not become a reality in the states dominated by migrants of European origins until very recently. In North America, for example, the early generations of Chinese sojourners who had to live among European colonists and migrants missed out on the upward social mobility that had long been available in Southeast Asia. In the Chinatowns of North America and Australasia, the

Chinese were slow to take the route of civic activity and political participation in order to enhance their positions. This was partly because they did not have the numbers, and partly because they had been demoralized by the discriminatory policies of the previous era.[8] They confined themselves to specific issues concerning themselves, such as immigration policies, their right to provide Chinese education, and their right to control their own media and their many social and cultural organizations. The "old *huaqiao*" had to wait for the diminution of their *huaqiao* patriotism and for their social betterment through local education before they gained enough confidence to involve themselves in problems affecting the national community. Also important was the rise of multiculturalism, a phenomenon I shall come back to.

CHOOSING NEW IDENTITIES

Third, many local-born Chinese, having succeeded in resisting both resinicization and localization pressures, chose to consider *new identities* for themselves. They had noted the growing gap between the Chinese ideal propounded by educational leaders in China and the reality of living with people of different cultural backgrounds and being influenced by the dominant majority culture. In addition, there were conflicting views regarding the nature of the modern Chinese identity. From the Chinese mainland, the new standards of revolutionary camaraderie after 1949 found little resonance elsewhere among most adult Chinese. There was greater sympathy for the ideals stressed by the Nationalist government in Taiwan, though not always credibly—pursuing a cultural continuity with what were deemed to be the values central to Chinese civilization. But the emphasis on traditional values had little appeal among the younger generation who had grown up in non-Chinese societies and had been educated in local schools and taught in national languages. It did not help that the differences between the rival claims of Taipei and Beijing to represent the true or new Chinese identity were politicized. This often resulted in more confusion than inspiration. For many of the local-born abroad, these claims became increasingly irrelevant in the rapidly changing local societies in which they lived.

What was nevertheless helpful was the change of policy by the Beijing government which Zhou Enlai made public when he went to the Bandung Conference in 1955. He began to encourage Chinese sojourners to settle down and become loyal citizens wherever they were. The People's Republic of China even developed a new terminology for them, calling such Chinese *waiji huaren* (foreign nationals of Chinese descent) in order to distinguish them from *guiqiao* (returned overseas Chinese sojourners) and to recognize the new realities.[9] Under such conditions, it was not surprising that many local-born individuals chose to consider new identities for themselves. This had become possible because of fundamental changes in attitudes toward assimilation and ethnicity in the migrant states of North America and Australia.

The 1950s still belonged to an age that believed in the assimilation of all immigrants. The melting pot model of the United States, expressed in Western social science scholarship of the time, was immensely influential in the new nation-states of Asia. Southeast Asian governments incorporated this model into their programs, and Chinese sojourners, especially the local-born, were told that their ultimate destiny was to merge totally into the new national identity. The first step for such Chinese was to consciously stop being sojourners and become normal migrants, that is, people who would settle in their countries and take up the citizenship offered to them. They had to choose between local commitment and returning to China or, if they liked neither, they could choose a third course and remigrate somewhere else. They had to face the question of what kind of Chinese they were, and some were led to ask whether they wanted to be identified as any kind of Chinese at all.

But, by the 1970s, the U.S. model of the melting pot had changed shape. The civil rights battle was largely won, and the slogans of equal opportunity and antidiscrimination had gained acceptance. Gradually there evolved a new goal of multiculturalism. Its ideals influenced other migrant states in the Americas and Australasia, but were not widely shared among the older nation-states in Western Europe and the newer nation-states in Southeast Asia. Chinese sojourners and immigrants everywhere took careful note of the new trends.

This multiculturalism initially created a new atmosphere of tolerance. It promoted stronger guarantees of legal rights, and these developments seemed to allow the return of some aspects of the earlier low-key and passive sojourning that existed before the communities were defined by China as patriotic *huaqiao*. It was not surprising that countries like the United States, Canada, and Australia, which officially adopted multicultural policies, were more open to Chinese immigration. And, when the latest era of migration began in the 1960s, the conditions in these states were favorable to a new generation of immigrants who now sought citizenship and naturalization in the host country from the outset.

Taiwan and Hong Kong migrants and Southeast Asian remigrating families led the way, but the most significant have been the hundreds of thousands from the Chinese mainland who have emigrated since the 1980s.[10] Paradoxically, the presence of the better educated, arriving from several different sources of migration, made it possible for ethnic Chinese communities to revitalize the standards of what it meant to be Chinese. The newcomers variously represented different sets of Chinese values that called for more self-awareness among earlier immigrants. This self-examination not only induced both newcomers and older Chinese residents to seek the core values that made them Chinese in one another's eyes, but also kept alive the earlier tradition of sojourning, that is, sojourning with the interventionist politics of China left out.[11]

But the challenge of modernity and multiculturalism also encouraged direct participation in local and national affairs, civic causes, politics, education, and science. Thus remaining culturally Chinese did not require hanging on to traditional values. On the contrary, the new Chinese identity was built on the growing confidence that communities could succeed in modernizing themselves outside China. Increasingly, this meant that they were ready to test their new ethnic identities in civic and political life. Multiculturalism provided acceptable avenues to show loyalty to their new homes.

Individuals were also able to search for their own personal place in their adopted homes.[12] Many found their own cultural amalgam or niche where they could assert their new identity. The internationally acclaimed works of ethnic Chinese novelists, playwrights, musicians, and film-makers in North America have symbolized this success. (Maxine Hong Kingston, Amy Tan, Henry David Hwang, and Wayne Wang, for example, have been seen as symbols for the new breed of modern Chinese, whether they intended to serve as such or not.) Elsewhere, in Southeast Asia, Australia, or Europe, artistic and literary outlets for Chinese minorities have been more parochial, but the urge to record the excitement of self-discovery has been no less exhilarating. The trend has been to turn away from previous concerns that hinged on what was or was not Chinese, how to stay close to some ideal type of Chinese, and even who was a better Chinese than others. Instead, there has developed a sense that the ability to digest what is modern, and what they have learned from their new homes, has helped each individual find his or her own voice as Chinese. This identity did not depend on whether they could read or write Chinese; many other cultural expressions of being Chinese were now possible and legitimate. These Chinese voices might eventually be seen as alternate ways of being modern Chinese that could even be relevant to the younger generations in China, Hong Kong, and Taiwan.[13]

BUSINESS AND EDUCATION

The fourth aspect of the story begins with the new generations of the local-born who were determined to settle down as distinctive ethnic groups in each country. Their numbers grew quickly. Their position between Chineseness and local assimilation produced a lifestyle that reminds us of the traditional sojourners prior to their politicization by China, but with important differences. Their numbers were further augmented by those China-born whose business aspirations and political views had turned them away from a China dominated by communist ideology. The emerging ethnic groups were further distinguished by the modern and professional education of their younger generations, among whom were those increasingly attracted to cosmopolitan and more global values. Their successes raised new questions concerning the nature of Chineseness itself.

The freedom experienced by Chinese outside China allowed them to concentrate on the twin pillars of seeking their fortunes and acquiring modern knowledge. Without the pressure to identify with political issues in China, most of the immigrants and their children turned their attention to business, education, and a range of social and cultural ways specific to their adopted homes. This reminds us again of the *peranakan* communities of Southeast Asia and the way in which they survived the period of the patriotic *huaqiao* earlier in this century. Two *peranakan* strategies were most effective: to be successful in business and the professions and to be able to master multicultural skills. The first enabled them to enjoy a measure of autonomy and make contributions to the local society. The second not only helped their business but also enriched their social life and made enduring friendships possible between them and the non-Chinese peoples among which they lived.

If one believes all that is written about the Chinese overseas today, it may seem that every one of them is a tycoon and millionaire, that the Chinese are born business geniuses, and that the whole economic transformation in Hong Kong, Taiwan, the People's Republic, and most of Southeast Asia has been their doing. Yet that is completely misleading, and the sensational reporting probably mischievous.[14] The story of the millions who remain poor is rarely reported on. And the fact that, until recently, wealth in itself was not a Chinese cultural value is also not understood. Nevertheless, given the shortage of upwardly mobile careers in public service open to those of Chinese descent in most countries, the importance of business for them cannot be overestimated. Not only was trade the major reason that the original sojourners evolved, but trade and more generally commercial expertise also provided the comparative advantage the Chinese had in countries that protected private enterprise.[15]

It is striking how miserable and unsuccessful the Chinese abroad were in communist and socialist countries like the Soviet Union and those in Eastern Europe, where people who showed their merchant-capitalist instincts had been penalized. Even in Southeast Asia itself, the contrast between socialist Burma and communist Vietnam on the one hand and the original countries of the Association of Southeast Asian Nations (ASEAN) on the other, is unmistakable. In the latter five countries, Thailand, Indonesia, Malaysia, the Philippines, and Singapore, business has been favored, and the entrepreneurial Chinese have made contributions to economic growth and are seen as valuable citizens. Indeed, it is true that these Chinese have had a disproportionate share of the private corporate wealth of each of those countries.[16] But clearly Chinese business people flourish only when the environment is right.

Furthermore, business today requires more than hard work, good luck, and entrepreneurial instincts. A business may be started that way but rarely can be maintained without something more. Modern education, which earlier generations of sojourners had not needed, has become increasingly important since World War II.

Here the local-born who have not been encumbered by patriotic *huaqiao* politics are better equipped. Mastery of the local language and, increasingly, of English as the international language of business and modern science, and familiarity with the mores of the majority community, are further strengthened by formal schooling in national schools. Data from every country where the Chinese are found show their commitment to education.

And as the local-born younger generations have acquired a modern and professional education, especially in business and in the technological fields, they have been able to take advantage of the dynamic growth of the global economy, especially the dramatic penetration of that economy into East and Southeast Asia since the 1970s. The tendency of so many of the younger generation to earn their MBAs from top universities in the United States is no accident. A steady move away from the *huaqiao* syndrome has prepared local-born Chinese to join with new immigrants to build new kinds of business networks that spread well beyond the region to Japan, the United States, and Europe. With their cross-cultural and multinational linkages in place, these ethnic Chinese minorities have learned to be less dependent on China's economy. But many have still kept their China connections alive, largely through Hong Kong. Thus when Deng Xiaoping's economic reforms came unexpectedly after 1978, they were ready to respond in both new and traditional ways.

FRESH MIGRATIONS

The fifth part of the story concerns *fresh migrations*. Unlike Southeast Asia, the migrant states of North America and Australia began to open their doors to steady and continuous Chinese immigration from the 1960s on. This included remigrants from Southeast Asia, and many who were much better educated and wealthier than ever in the past. By the 1980s, the large number of first-generation Chinese in Canada, the United States, and Australia was contributing to an emerging multicultural environment.

The United States began admitting Chinese from Taiwan and the mainland soon after 1949, including large numbers of students from Taiwan, while other migrant states began to open their doors to Chinese immigration in the 1960s. The newcomers came as whole families and, although most of them were aware that they were immigrants planning to settle down in their host country, they behaved remarkably like the traditional sojourners who wanted to protect their Chinese identity abroad. Some of the remigrants from Southeast Asia had chosen the migrant states precisely because they thought those nations' tolerance, ethnic rights, and style of life could help them conserve the Chinese qualities and values they still believed in.

Because those in the new wave were often much better educated than in the past, the chances of their preserving their Chinese ways were also greater. Given in addition the ease of communications, the possibility of affordable regular visits to Chinese territories, and the accessibility of Chinese books, magazines, films, and the electronic media, the sojourning mentality could much more easily be supported. The new multiculturalism in these countries also provided much encouragement. By the 1980s, the large numbers of newly arrived first-generation Chinese were themselves enriching that multicultural environment. The fact that they included numbers of engineers, scientists, mathematicians, professionals, and academics in a wide range of disciplines suggests that the impact will be even greater in the near future.

Does this mean that the Chinese will now become settlers, and that remaining Chinese through the tradition of sojourning has finally come to an end? Paradoxically, ease of communication and global mobility has made the sojourning attitude easier to sustain. Like the wealthy and the professional classes in Europe who never saw themselves as migrants, the successful Chinese from the same classes behave in similar ways. They are now internationally mobile, people who travel extensively and freely sojourn. A practice common among Hong Kong migrants, for example, given the name of "astronaut syndrome," has developed among families that are separated because of sojourning conditions. The "astronaut," or breadwinner, leaves his wife and children behind in the place of sojourn while he flies back and forth to Hong Kong to continue with his business. For other Chinese, only the direction of sojourning has changed. They are not necessarily sojourning from China, but sojourning from wherever they have previously called home.[17]

In sharp contrast, Chinese immigration into Southeast Asia virtually ended in the 1950s. At the end of World War II, 90 percent of all overseas Chinese lived in the region; in the 1990s, the figure was down to about 80 percent. Of this 80 percent, most were local-born and were less knowledgeable about China than their parents were. Few would ever think of returning to live in China. As a result, the national governments of the region have become less concerned about their loyalties. Doing business with China promises to be ongoing indefinitely. Some of these governments have begun to recognize the value of being familiar with China, and even encourage their own peoples to learn and master the Chinese language.

For the Chinese in the region, China is proximate. Increasingly, they trade and invest there, they travel and learn there, and their involvement with China grows. Even without fresh immigration into the region, these relationships could deepen. With a solid foundation in economic ties and with Chinese entrepreneurial capacity attaining new heights, there is also renewed interest in modern Chinese culture. It should be no surprise if there develops among some Chinese a rekindling of their concern for a higher degree of Chineseness.

A NEW SEAWARD-LOOKING CHINA?

What of China and its policies toward the seaward sweep of its people? China's recent economic transformation has led to much speculation about its potential power in the region, even causing some alarm among its neighbors. Popular books and articles refer constantly to Greater China, to the rise of Chinese nationalism, to China's claims in the Spratly Islands, to China's readiness to resort to military action to achieve its goals, and so on. Will these new developments radically change Chinese attitudes toward a more maritime China? If the picture of a China threat continues to bring concern to its neighbors, what role is there for the Chinese overseas? Is history any guide?

In Chapter 1, I described the most successful period for the overseas Chinese before modern times as that of the seventeenth century, when there were three conditions that enabled the Hokkiens of southern Fujian to achieve unprecedented success. The three conditions were

1. A weakened central government in Beijing, which allowed the coastal provinces to engage directly in foreign trade.
2. The pulling back of Japanese activity, which left the Chinese with no other Asian rivals.
3. The fierce rivalry between the Dutch and the Spanish, which gave the Chinese privateers room to maneuver.

The first condition in a new form has existed to large degree since the 1980s. Will it be reversed when centralized power is strengthened? Will the continental mind-set be reestablished in Beijing? I think not, certainly not intentionally. It is recognized that today the sea lanes and the world of container ships are where the wealth is coming from. China's strategy to develop the coastal provinces first before moving deeper into the interior is a firm commitment. The infrastructural investments on the coast are so extensive that the traditional mind-set can be said to have changed, much more so than is realized by the world outside. A severe test of this change will come as China handles Hong Kong as its new Special Administrative Region. Eventually the central government will seek a better balance between coast and interior and will offer the interior provinces more help, but this will not come at the expense of continued prosperity along the coasts. Given that condition, the future for the ethnic Chinese in Southeast Asia, with whom the coastal provinces trade most closely, should be one of increased intimacy in the long run.

The second condition does not exist. Although China does not have another obvious rival in Asia other than Japan, Japan is very much an active protagonist. But this is not a zero sum situation. In a global market economy based on openness, a maritime industrial and trading power like Japan would be a major asset to all of coastal China. In addition, there are now other players, South Korea, Taiwan, and several of the Southeast Asian states, all of whom still have the capacity to stimulate China's continued economic growth. And not least, the Chinese overseas in all these areas have facilitated deepening economic ties between China and Japan as well as with other neighbors. These Chinese will be able to do a great deal more with their investments and technology transfers.

The third condition of rivalry between major powers on the China coast may be compared with the U.S.-Soviet cold war before 1989. That struggle for power and influence helped the Chinese in Southeast Asia to master the skills of industrial and financial capitalism and build their entrepreneurial networks. In addition, the rivalry also helped China take great strides into the global market economy in the 1980s. This condition too no longer exists, but could an analogy be found in the economic rivalry between Japan and the United States? This is unlikely to turn into a serious conflict. If it occurs, it could only further stimulate China's future maritime commitments. But the geopolitics of the region are so sensitive, especially in Northeast Asia and including the United States and Russia, that any conflict between the major protagonists would do untold damage to every country's economic development. If there is a new danger to be identified, it lies elsewhere, possibly in a direct confrontation between China and the United States, which many U.S. strategists and journalists seem to look forward to.[18] The ethnic Chinese who have settled in the United States and allied countries need not be a liability. Their growing numbers, especially in North America, will ensure their vested interest in helping to maintain and expand areas of cooperation between their host countries and China. Such a task, of course, requires sensitivity to, and finesse in handling, the local political culture. Clumsily done, efforts on China's behalf could backfire and bring back an atmosphere of suspicion and hostility toward the Chinese overseas.[19]

The key to peace and stability in the region lies in China's attitudes toward the maritime linkages that have been established during the past century. For two millennia, China had only overland enemies. At the time of the Opium War, Britain and other maritime powers posed a challenge to China's continental mindset. Today, the only superpower, the United States, is both continental and maritime. This status has helped it to succeed the maritime British, on the one hand, and gain clear superiority over the continental Russians and Germans, on the other. For China in the twentieth century, the powerful shadow of the Soviet Union has been continental while Japan has been the maritime threat. Is China finally ready to redefine itself to give equal weight to its maritime interests? Deng Xiaoping's wish to have his ashes scattered over the seas may be symbolic of that change.[20] If China adds a commitment to look seaward to its continental history and geography, it could become the counterweight to the United States in the western Pacific. China could also accomplish this if Japan were its close and permanent ally, but even that would require it to develop a more maritime view of global politics.

How do China's growing maritime concerns relate to its attitudes and policies toward the Chinese overseas, toward the tradition of sojourning and the cultural autonomy of the foreign nationals of Chinese descent? How will that develop eventually?

Since 1949 the decisive change has been China's remarkable opening after thirty years' of hostility toward the capitalist world. During that earlier, closed period, reflecting the traditional continental mind-set, the concept of China as a future Great Power politically and ideologically was always present in the region, but a business-minded China was not. China's isolation forced the Chinese overseas to look to their own resources. Many were more than willing to assimilate locally, but were constantly reminded of their Chinese heritage by dominant majorities as well as by their own communities. Most of the migrants fell back on old strategies of cultural maintenance. Their success in extending their entrepreneurial networks, and in building new ones to meet new challenges, was greatly helped by the vital role of other Chinese on the periphery, in Hong Kong and Taiwan, who were not held down by the continental pull.

Other contributing factors were the cold war concerns of the United States, which made the region a front line for capitalism, and the remarkable recovery of Japanese industrialization after the war. American guarantees in Japan and South Korea, its special support for Taiwan, and its willingness to go to war against communism in Vietnam provided additional opportunities for the Chinese in the region to create business space for themselves in innovative ways. In addition, Anglo-Australian defense commitments enabled Malaysia and Singapore to develop a pivotal role for themselves in anchoring the export-led strategies that transformed the regional economy. Stable leadership in both these countries under the United Malay National Organisation (UMNO) and the People's Action Party (PAP), respectively, as well as in Indonesia under President Suharto, provided the environment that their nationals of Chinese descent needed. Whether this degree of trust and acceptance can continue if the financial crisis in Asia since July 1997 becomes a protracted one will be a major challenge for Chinese adaptability and resilience. This will be a subject that deserves close scrutiny for years to come.[21]

It was in this context that China returned after 1978 to become an active economic player after a lapse of thirty years. At the beginning, PRC officials, including those who specialized in *huaqiao* affairs, found the Chinese overseas cautious and unresponsive, because most Chinese had been greatly dismayed by the disastrous decade of the Cultural Revolution. Although they welcomed Deng Xiaoping's economic reforms, most of them had little faith in their effectiveness. Those who still had family in China wanted to resume contacts with their relatives, but found that many, including those patriotic Chinese who had returned to China in the 1950s, had suffered harshly and unnecessarily during the years of chaos and deprivation. The office of *huaqiao* affairs was revived by Liao Chengzhi, and its heritage carefully guarded by a generation loyal to the faith that Sun Yat-sen had kept with the *huaqiao* since 1911.[22] Whether inside or outside China, there were sharply divided views as to what should be done with that historic connection. At the same time, this was not a priority matter. There were many more urgent issues for China in the international arena as China opened its doors for investment and allowed its best and brightest to go abroad to study. The exhilarating events of the first decade after 1978 dwarfed concerns about the China-*huaqiao* relationship. When no one was certain what best to do, it seemed wisest to let the open door policy take its course, with a minimum of intervention by the central government.

This openness provided the most effective answer to the question of how to maintain links with the new generations of foreign Chinese who had chosen to live abroad. The role of Hong Kong was crucial. Its proximity to and familiarity with the provinces of Guangdong and Fujian, where most Chinese abroad had come from, made the territory the vital link. From there, ties were restored, donations to home villages and institutions like schools and ancestral temples were made, and with them came the first tentative investments to enable relatives to launch themselves in business in China's unfolding market-oriented economy. Eventually, careful understandings were reached between the governments of China and Southeast Asia regarding the ways in which foreign nationals of Chinese descent might help to deepen the commercial relations that were rapidly growing between themselves and China.

As for the concept of sojourning, Hong Kong and Taiwan each made their own contribution. During the years of the PRC's isolation, emigrants from Hong Kong and Taiwan to North America and Australasia experienced the new emphasis on cultural autonomy in their host countries, and built strong links with their families at home. Most of them had migrated because of uncertainty over the future of the two territories, and the instinct to sojourn was revived as new technology was harnessed for cultural maintenance. This kept open the prospect of returning home sometime in the future, when conditions improved. A new version of sojourning was in place. Of course, now that Hong Kong has become part of China again, the situation may change somewhat. More recently, a similar attitude has been found among emigrants from the mainland of China as well. As the old sojourners have largely settled into their new homes and become foreign nationals of Chinese descent, the new sojourners, mainly from China and other Chinese territories, have taken their place. What impact this will have, if any, on the settlers who have chosen to integrate themselves into their local societies is something that will be most interesting to watch.

The evidence of history is that overseas Chinese communities have always sought as much cultural autonomy as they could get wherever they have gone. This was relatively easy before the modern nation-states demanded assimilation from their minorities. In the face of that, the ethnic Chinese have modified their goals and marked out their areas of cultural space in the countries that allowed it. Some have remigrated in search of such space elsewhere. Now that assimilationist policies have softened in the face of multicultural alternatives, the greater autonomy which that promises will encourage ever more immigrant Chinese to become loyal to the countries that have offered them acceptance under culturally favorable terms. How long this will remain, and how it will affect generations of the local-born, and the local-born to come, is unknown. Many variables are involved in the formation of Chinese communities overseas. With so many unpredictable elements to be taken into account, this will be a subject of intense and enduring interest. The only prediction I am prepared to make is that, given the willingness of more countries to see themselves as multicultural, given the Chinese tradition of sojourning, and given the massive presence of a China that is finally turning seaward, there will always be some ethnic Chinese who will press for the autonomy they need in order to remain culturally Chinese as long as possible.

Notes

Index

Notes

ONE *Seaward Sweep*

1. Owen Lattimore's masterly study, *Inner Asian Frontiers of China* (New York: American Geographical Society, 1940; 2nd ed., 1951; new edition with an introduction by Alastair Lamb, 1988), explores this theme thoroughly.

2. The peoples, tribes, and tribal groups in southern and southwest China are clustered under the name of Yue. Some were on the verge of statehood before the Qin unification during the third century B.C. They have been recently studied with the help of archaeological discoveries. Most of those who originated in southeastern China have been assimilated by Han Chinese from the north through the millennia. Until these peoples can be accurately identified, most scholars fall back on the traditional designation for them as the Baiyue, "Hundred Yue." Their better-known descendants survive mainly in the southwest. Those who are still distinct from the Han Chinese are the Yao, Miao, Yi, Zhuang, Li, Dai, and the Vietnamese. You Zhong, *Zhongguo Xinan minzu shi* (History of the peoples of Southwest China) (Kunming: Yunnan People's Publishers, 1985); Zhu Junming, ed., *Bai Yue shi yanjiu*

(Research on the history of the Hundred Yuehs) (Guiyang, Guizhou: Guizhou People's Publisher, 1987).

3. The earliest reference to Xu Fu, the astrologer who was ordered by Qin Shihuangdi (First Emperor, 246–210 B.C.) to sail eastward in search of longevity plants, is found in Sima Qian's *Shiji* (Historical records), completed early in the first century B.C. Centuries later, it was speculated that he and the thousands of young men and women who traveled with him settled in Japan. Numerous claims this century that Xu Fu established a community around Saga on Kyushu Island have been disputed. The most enthusiastic supporter of this idea in Japan has been Nakata Ken, president of the Xu Fu Society. More scholars have pursued this idea in Hong Kong, Taiwan, and mainland China, notably Wei Tingsheng in *Xu Fu ru Riben jianguo kao* (Xu Fu established a state in Japan: a study) in 1950–51, which views Nakata Ken accepted (in *Xu Fu yu Riben*, Hong Kong: New Era Press, 1953). A more recent summary of the debates may be found in Yu Jinghong, *Xu Fu dongdu zhi mi xintan* (A new examination of Xu Fu's voyage to the east) (Nanjing: Jiangsu People's Publishing, 1990).

4. The following account up to the tenth century draws on my study *The Nanhai Trade: The Early History of Chinese Trade in the South China Sea*, new ed. (Singapore: Times Academic Press, 1998). This was first completed in 1954 and published in the *Journal of the Malayan Branch of the Royal Asiatic Society*, 31, pt. 2 (1958): 1–135.

5. These terms have now been shown to have been used, in most cases in this early period, to refer to things and

peoples pertaining to the Southeast Asian region. There has been considerable confusion about the *bosi*, particularly in later Chinese sources, where Southeast Asian data have been placed together with material on the Persians. The debates concerning the identification of *bosi* and *kunlun* have gone on for more than a century. The best summary of the arguments is to be found in O. W. Wolters, *Early Indonesian Commerce: A Study of the Origins of Srivijaya* (Ithaca, N.Y.: Cornell University Press, 1967), pp. 129–158.

6. This is well documented by Oliver Wolters in his book *Early Indonesian Commerce.*

7. I should add that my first encounter with Professor Reischauer's scholarship was with his two volumes on the monk Ennin, who traveled from Japan to China in the ninth century. Reischauer gave me insight into the nature of early Sino-Japanese relations that has helped me to compare the relations that China had with Southeast Asia. Edwin O. Reischauer, *Ennin's Diary: The Record of a Pilgrimage to China in Search of the Law* and *Ennin's Travels in T'ang China* (New York: Ronald Press, 1955).

8. Edward H. Schafer studied two of these empires in conjunction with his erudite studies of T'ang images of the outside world. They are remarkable in that they take fuller account of China's early openness to the maritime world than most studies of the T'ang, which consistently give precedence to overland relations with central and western Asia. See Schafer, "The History of the Empire of Southern Han according to Chapter 65 of the Wu Tai Shih of Ouyang Hsiu," in *Silver Jubilee Volume of the Jimbun Kagaku Kenkyuso*

(Kyoto: Kyoto University, 1954); *The Empire of Min* (Tokyo: Kodansha, 1959); *The Golden Peaches of Samarkand: A Study of T'ang Exotics* (Berkeley: University of California Press, 1963); and *The Vermilion Bird: T'ang Images of the South.* (Berkeley: University of California Press, 1967).

9. Paul Wheatley, "Geographical Notes on Some Commodities Involved in Sung Maritime Trade," *Journal of the Malayan Branch of the Royal Asiatic Society*, 32, pt. 2 (1959): 1–140, illustrates the extent of Song China's overseas trade.

10. F. Hirth and W. W. Rockhill, *Chau Ju-kua: His Work on the Chinese and Arab Trade in the 12th and 13th centuries, Entitled Chu-Fan-Chih* (St. Petersburg: Imperial Academy of Science, 1911).

11. Wang Dayuan's work was largely translated by W. W. Rockhill: "Notes on the Relations and Trade of China with the Eastern Archipelago and the Coasts of the Indian Ocean during the Fourteenth Century," *T'oung Pao* (1914–1915), vol. 15, pp. 419–447; vol. 16, pp. 61–159, 234–271, 374–392, 435–467, 604–626.

12. Postface in *Daoyi zhilue jiaoshi (A Brief Record of Island Barbarians)* (Beijing: Zhonghua, 1981), p. 385.

13. Zhou Daguan, *Zhenla fongtu ji jiaozhu* (An annotated adition of Zhenla fongtu ji), with annotations by Xia Nai (Beijing: Zhonghua, 1981). There is a specific reference which suggests that the Chinese began to settle in Cambodia during the Yuan dynasty, pp. 180–181. Many more Chinese were settled further south in the Malay Archipelago by the end of the Yuan, as evidenced in the records of the Zheng He expeditions; *Ma Huan: Ying-yai Sheng-lan. The Overall*

Survey of the Ocean's Shores [1433], trans. and ed. J. V. G. Mills (Cambridge: Cambridge University Press, 1970). See also *Oeuvres posthumes de Paul Pelliot*, "Mémoires sur les coutumes du Cambodge de Tcheou Ta-Kouan, version nouvelle suivie d'un commentaire inachevé," vol. 3 (Paris: Libraire d'Amérique et d'Orient, Adrien-Maisoneuve, 1951); and the studies on this text by the historical geographer Ch'en Cheng-hsiang, *Zhenla fongtu ji yanjiu* (Studies on the Zhenla fongtu ji) (Hong Kong: Chinese University Press, 1975.)

14. Zhu Xi (1130–1200), whose Neo-Confucianism "dominated China for seven hundred years" was born in Fujian and lived there for more than sixty-five years; his pervasive influence led to a long tradition of loyal followers, including many from southern Fujian; Wing-tsit Chan, *Chu Hsi: Life and Thought* (Hong Kong: Chinese University Press, 1987), and Gao Lingyin and Chen Qifang, *Fujian Zhuxi xue* (Zhu Xi learning in Fujian) (Fuzhou: Fujian Renmin Publishers, 1986). These generations of disciples provided a sharp contrast to the strong image of the adventurous, seafaring, and entrepreneurial fellow provincials known in Southeast Asia as the Hokkiens.

15. Most clans of Fujian and Guangdong, notably those who trace their ancestries to the Tang and Song dynasties, take great pride in their origins from provinces like Henan and others in the north-central plains. The local gazetteers also tend to stress the blood ties and cultural links with north-central China.

16. Where Southeast Asia was concerned, references to Chinese traders and settlers may be found in many

contemporary Chinese sources; see Wang Gungwu's essays on this period collected in *Community and Nation: Essays on Southeast Asia and the Chinese*, selected by Anthony Reid (Singapore and Sydney: Heinemann Educational Books (Asia) and George Allen & Unwin Australia, 1981), pp. 58–107. More recent studies are Chang Pin-tsun, "The First Chinese Diaspora in Southeast Asia in the Fifteenth Century," in *Emporia, Commodities, and Entrepreneurs in Asian Maritime Trade, c. 1400–1750*, ed. Roderich Ptak and Dietmar Rothermund (Stuttgart: Franz Steiner Verlag, 1991), pp. 13–38; and Anthony Reid, "Flows and Seepages in the Long-Term Chinese Interaction with Southeast Asia," in *Sojourners and Settlers: Histories of Southeast Asia and the Chinese*, ed. Anthony Reid (Sydney: Allen & Unwin, 1996), pp. 15–49. The most complete documentation is found in the translations of all accounts relating to Southeast Asia in the *Ming Shilu* by Geoffrey Philip Wade and submitted as a Ph.D. thesis to the University of Hong Kong in 1994: "The *Ming Shi-lu* (Veritable Records of the Ming Dynasty) as a Source for Southeast Asian History—4th to 17th Centuries," 8 vols., with index in vol. VIII.

17. The debate as to whether the Wako (*wokou*) were mainly Japanese or Chinese pirates has swung back and forth, but there has never been any doubt that the most active on the coasts of Zhejiang, Fujian, and Guangdong included local armed merchants. See So Kwan-wai, *Japanese Piracy in Ming China during the Sixteenth Century* (East Lansing: Michigan State University Press, 1975). Among many recent Chinese studies, Lin Renchuan's *Mingmo Qingchu siren haishang*

maoyi (Shanghai: Huadong Shifan Daxue Press, 1987) is the most thorough.

18. This was the dominant view. Yu Ying-shih has demonstrated that there were significant efforts by Ming and Qing scholars to challenge this prejudice; *Chung-kuo chin-shih tsung-chiao lun-li yu shang-jen ching-shen* (Religious ethics and the merchant spirit in China's recent history) (Taipei: Lian-ching Publishers, 1987); and "Business Culture and Chinese Traditions—Toward a Study of the Evolution of Merchant Culture in Chinese History," in *Dynamic Hong Kong: Business and Culture*, ed. Wang Gungwu and Wong Siu-lun (Hong Kong: Centre of Asian Studies, University of Hong Kong, 1997), pp. 1–84.

TWO *The Sojourners' Way*

1. Wang Gungwu, "Migration and Its Enemies," in *Conceptualizing Global History*, ed. Bruce Mazlish and Ralph Buultjens (Boulder: Westview Press, 1993), pp. 131–151; Wang Gungwu, "Sojourning: The Chinese Experience in Southeast Asia," in *Sojourners and Settlers: Histories of Southeast Asia and the Chinese*, ed. Anthony Reid (Sydney: Allen & Unwin, 1996), pp. 1–14.

2. Michael Godley, "The Late Ch'ing Courtship of the Chinese in Southeast Asia," *Journal of Asian Studies*, 34, no. 2 (1975): 361–385.

3. Wang Gungwu, "The Origins of Hua-Ch'iao," in *Community and Nation: China, Southeast Asia, and Australia*, new ed. (Sydney: Allen & Unwin, 1992), pp. 1–10.

4. Zhang Xie's original studies of the countries of the "eastern and western oceans" was published in 1617 and were the main sources for many studies for the next two centuries; republished as *Dong xiyang kao* in Taipei by Cheng Chung Bookshop, 1962. The project to have the whole work translated has been undertaken by Leonard Blusse and his colleagues at Leiden University in collaboration with scholars at Xiamen University. A recent study that shows how far afield Chinese traders in search of exotic commodities had gone in the Malay Archipelago by the end of the sixteenth century is Stephen Tseng-Hsin Chang, "Commodities Imported to the Chang-chou Region of Fukien during the Late Ming Period: A Preliminary Analysis of the Tax Lists Found in *Tung-hsi-yang k'ao*," in *Emporia, Commodities, and Entrepreneurs in Asian Maritime Trade, c. 1400–1750*, ed. Roderick Ptak and Dietmar Rothermund (Stuttgart: Franz Steiner Verlag, 1991), pp. 159–194.

5. The *Haiguo wenjianlu* was completed in 1730. The author, Chen Lunjiong, drew from his father's experience of trading in Southeast Asia in the 1670s and 1680s and supplemented that with his own inquiries among foreign merchants. Father and son both became coastal defense officials. The book was primarily concerned with the countries from which the foreign merchants came rather than with the Chinese merchants who traded with them. For example, Chen Lunjiong's knowledge of the Malays and their relations with the Dutch and the Spanish was extensive; Wang Gungwu, "The Melayu in Hai-kuo wen-chien lu," in *Community and Nation: Essays on Southeast Asia and the Chinese*, selected by

Anthony Reid (Singapore and Sydney: Heinemann Educational Books (Asia) and George Allen & Unwin Australia, 1981), pp. 108–117.

6. Wang Dahai lived in Java from 1783 and completed this work in 1791, but the earliest edition appeared only in 1806. It is not clear how long he was in Java altogether, but probably less than ten years. In his case, he actually lived with a wealthy Chinese family in Semarang and knew a great deal about the lifestyle of rich Chinese living among the Dutch and the Javanese. His work was translated into English in the nineteenth century: Ong Tae-hae, *The Chinaman Abroad, or a Desultory Account of the Malayan Archipelago, particularly of Java*, ed. and trans. W. H. Medhurst (Shanghai: Mission Press, 1849). A recent annotated edition of the original *Haidao yizhi* was published in the historical rare documents series produced by the Chinese University of Hong Kong and the Overseas Chinese History Society of Shanghai, annotations by Yao Nan and Wu Langxuan (Hong Kong: Xuejin Book Store, 1992).

7. Xie Qinggao's *Hai lu* was recorded by Yang Bingnan in 1820. He had gone blind in 1796 at the age of thirty-one. By that time, he had been sailing in the southern seas for fourteen years. The excellent annotated edition completed by Feng Chengjun in 1936 was republished in 1955: *Hai lu zhu* (Beijing: Zhonghua).

8. The different fates of these and other creole societies have been well described by G. William Skinner. His seminal essay was "Change and Persistence in Chinese Culture Overseas: A Comparison of Thailand and Java," *Journal of*

the South Seas Society, 16 (1960): 86–100. He has continued to refine and expand its scope, and his recent study, "Creolized Chinese Societies in Southeast Asia," is authoritative; in *Sojourners and Settlers: Histories of Southeast Asia and the Chinese*, ed. Anthony Reid (Sydney: Allen & Unwin, 1996), pp. 51–93.

9. Robert Lee Irick, "Ch'ing Policy toward the Coolie Trade, 1847–1878," Ph.D. thesis, Harvard University, 1971, 2 vols. A later version was published as *Ch'ing Policy toward the Coolie Trade* (Taipei: Chinese Materials Centre, 1982).

10. There are many scholarly studies of nineteenth-century Chinese migration around the world that bring out one or more of the features summarized here. The collection of documents that captures all aspects of the phenomenon is the eleven-volume work edited by Chen Hansheng et al., *Huagong chuguo shiliao* (Beijing: Zhonghua Publishers, 1980–1985).

11. Xue Fucheng (1838–1894) was the minister to France, Great Britain, Belgium, and Italy from 1890 to 1894. His diaries of his years in Europe and other notes on foreign affairs were collected in his complete works, the *Yung-an ch'uan-chi*, completed in 1898. Huang Zunxian (1848–1905) began a diplomatic career at a relatively young age in Japan (1877–1882). He was consul-general in San Francisco (1882–1885), counselor in the legation in Britain (1890–1891), and consul-general in Singapore (1891–1894). He was particularly knowledgeable about the two kinds of overseas Chinese communities represented by Singapore (Southeast Asian) and San Francisco (migrant societies of North America). Zheng Guanying (1842–1921) is best known for his *Shengshi*

weiyan (Words of warning to an affluent age), a collection of essays written in the late nineteenth century that reflected the views of a new generation of modern businessmen in Hong Kong and Shanghai. His was one of the strongest voices speaking on the importance on trade and industry, and he showed considerable understanding of the entrepreneurial spirit among overseas Chinese.

12. The fullest study of Sun Yat-sen in London in 1896, and the subsequent impact of that fateful event, is J. Y. Wong, *The Origins of an Heroic Image: Sun Yat-sen in London, 1896–1897* (Hong Kong: Oxford University Press, 1986).

13. The public careers of the reformers Kang Youwei (1858–1927) and Liang Qichao (1873–1929) and their efforts to modernize the Qing government in 1898 have been well studied; see Hsiao Kung-ch'üan, *A Modern China and a New World: Kang Yu-wei, Reformer and Utopian* (Seattle: University of Washington Press, 1975, and Philip Huang, *Liang Ch'i-ch'ao and Modern Chinese Liberalism* (Seattle: University of Washington Press, 1972). The impact they had on overseas Chinese communities around the world is less well known, especially Kang's on education and cultural reform, and Liang's on all aspects of intellectual enlightenment, including his attention to the history of overseas Chinese activities that had been much neglected before the twentieth century.

14. This was one of two revolutionary doggerels published together with the very popular and influential work by Zou Rong (Tsou Jung) called *Geming jun* (Revolutionary Army) in 1903. My translation of an extract from that "song"

is appended to a paper originally written in 1976 for the festschrift for C. R. Boxer, "A Note on the Origins of *Hua-ch'iao*," *Masalah-Masalah Internasional Masakini*, ed. Lie Tek Tjeng, vol. 7 (Jakarta: Lembaga Research Kebudayaan Nasional, L.I.P.I., 1977), pp. 71–78; and reprinted in my 1981 collection, *Community and Nation: Essays on Southeast Asia and the Chinese*, selected by Anthony Reid (Singapore and Sydney: Heinemann Educational Books (Asia) and George Allen & Unwin Australia), pp. 118–127.

15. The books and articles published by the team of scholars of Jinan University of Shanghai in the 1920s and 1930s may be found in Hsu Yun-ch'iao, "Preliminary Bibliography of Southeast Asian Studies," *Nanyang yanjiu Bulletin*, no. 1 (1959): 1–169; see Austin C. W. Shu and William W. L. Wan, *Twentieth Century Chinese Works on Southeast Asia: A Bibliography* (Honolulu: East-West Center, 1968).

16. The *Nanyo kakyo sosho* (Nanyang Chinese Series) in six volumes published by the Toa Keizai Chosakyoku in Tokyo, 1939–1941, provides useful bibliographic data about the scope of Japanese research on the overseas Chinese. This is supplemented by the *Kakyo kankei bunken mokuroku* (Catalogue of documents concerning the overseas Chinese), published by Ajia Keizai Kenkyujo in 1973. More recently, see Yang Chien-chen and George L. Hicks, eds., *A Bibliography of Japanese Works on the Overseas Chinese in Southeast Asia, 1914–1945* (Hong Kong: Asian Research Service, 1992). The breadth of Japanese interest in Southeast Asia during this period can be seen in Chou Wan-yao and Tsung-hsien Tsai, eds., *Taiwan Shih-pao Tung-nan-ya tzu-liao mu-lu*

(1909–1945) (A catalogue of materials related to Southeast Asia in *The Taiwan Jiho*) (Taipei: Academia Sinica Program for Southeast Asian Area Studies, 1997).

17. Some sets of the textbooks published in Shanghai for use in *huaqiao* schools throughout the world before World War II may still be found in libraries outside China, but few are complete. For contemporary discussions of these textbooks, see Tsang Chiu-sam, *Nationalism in School Education in China* (Hong Kong: Progressive Education Publishers, 1967), first published in 1933; and Victor Purcell, *Problems of Chinese Education* (London: Kegan Paul, Trench and Truber, 1936).

THREE *The Multicultural Quest for Autonomy*

1. This sentiment is well described in Victor Purcell, *The Chinese in Southeast Asia* (1951; 2nd ed., 1965), introduction. One idea was that the Chinese overseas were a "fifth column" for China. Other ideas were captured in the following phrases: "an aggressive nationalism whose virtual claim was 'where there are Chinese, there is China'"; and "the attempts of the Kuomintang to form an *imperium in imperio* in each of the Southeast Asian countries," p. xi.

2. This kind of assimilation occurred more in mainland Southeast Asia and the Philippines. Elsewhere, creolization at all levels of society may be seen; see G. William Skinner, "Creolised Chinese Societies in Southeast Asia," in *Sojourners and Settlers: Histories of Southeast Asia and the Chinese*, ed. Anthony Reid (Sydney: Allen & Unwin, 1996), pp. 51–93.

Other degrees of assimilation are found in the two neighboring Indonesian islands of Bangka and Belitung, where the differences are significant; see Mary F. Somers Heidhues, *Bangka Tin and Mentok Pepper: Chinese Settlement on an Indonesian Island* (Singapore: Institute of Southeast Asian Studies, 1992), pp. 222–226.

3. The classic study that reflects the outlook of a *peranakan* most consistently is Song Ong Siang, *One Hundred Years' History of the Chinese in Singapore* (1923; Singapore: University of Malaya Press, 1967). Post–World War II research on the local-born began with the work of Maurice Freedman, "Colonial Law and Chinese Society," *Journal of the Royal Anthropological Institute of Great Britain and Ireland*, no. 80 (1950): 97–126. Two more recent studies are John R. Clammer, *Straits Chinese Society: Studies in the Sociology of the Baba Communities of Malaysia and Singapore* (Singapore: Singapore University Press, 1980); and Tan Chee Beng, *The Baba of Melaka: Culture and Identity of a Chinese Peranakan Community in Malaysia* (Petaling Jaya: Pelanduk Publications, 1988). For the *peranakan* of Indonesia, the steady series of essays by Claudine Salmon on the cultural life of the communities during the formative period, is authoritative; the bulk of the essays have been published in the journal *Archipel* (Paris), since 1971. Other valuable studies are Leo Suryadinata, *Peranakan Chinese Politics in Java* (Singapore: Institute of Southeast Asian Studies, 1976); Donald Willmott, *The Chinese of Semarang: A Changing Minority Community in Indonesia* (Ithaca, N.Y.: Cornell University Press,

1960); and Mely G. Tan, *The Chinese of Sukabumi: A Study in Social and Cultural Accommodation* (Ithaca, N.Y.: Cornell University Southeast Asia Program, 1963). A recent collection of essays on prominent *peranakan* Chinese is Leo Suryadinata, *Peranakan's Search for National Identity: Biographical Studies of Seven Indonesian Chinese* (Singapore: Times Academic Press, 1993).

4. I have long resisted the use of *diaspora* to describe the Chinese overseas, and am still concerned that it could acquire political overtones similar to those of *huaqiao*, which governments both inside and outside China have highlighted in the past (see note 1). In recent years, the term has been extended to cover almost every migrant community in the world and is now much diluted and variegated in connotation. I have explored how this might make the word more usable for the Chinese in Wang Gungwu, "A Single Chinese Diaspora?" inaugural lecture at the foundation of the Centre for the Study of the Chinese Southern Diaspora, Australian National University, Canberra, February 1999, in *Imagining the Chinese Diaspora: Two Australian Perspectives* (Canberra: CSCSD, ANU, 1999), pp. 1–17. See also Wang Ling-chi and Wang Gungwu, eds., *The Chinese Diaspora: Selected Essays*, 2 vols. (Singapore: Times Academic Press, 1998).

5. The wartime experience with the Japanese is succinctly described by the former prime minister of Singapore, Lee Kuan Yew, in the first volume of his autobiography, *The Singapore Story: Memoirs of Lee Kuan Yew* (Singapore: Times Editions, 1998), pp. 25–98. The general background is most

clearly provided in Willard H. Elsbree, *Japan's Role in South-East Asian Nationalist Movements* (Cambridge, Mass.: Harvard University Press, 1953).

6. Charles Coppel, *Indonesian Chinese in Crisis* (Kuala Lumpur: Oxford University, 1983). The cultural background of these Chinese is well depicted in a series of essays by Leo Suryadinata, *The Culture of the Chinese Minority in Indonesia* (Singapore: Times Books International, 1997). Geoff Forrester and R. J. May, eds., *The Fall of Soeharto* (London: C. Hurst, 1998), outline the specific circumstances that determined the fate of the Chinese in 1997–1998. For a wider perspective of the conditions under which the Chinese in Indonesia had seemed to prosper in the years before the disaster, Adam Schwarz, *A Nation in Waiting: Indonesia in the 1990s* (Boulder: Westview, 1994). The republication of the collection of short essays by Indonesia's most famous novelist, Promoedya Ananta Toer, *Hoakiau di Indonesia* (The Chinese in Indonesia) (Jakarta: Garba Budaya, 1998), reminds us of what might have been. This was first published in 1960 and banned; Wang Gungwu, "Ethnic Chinese: The Past in Their Future," keynote lecture at the International Conference on Ethnic Chinese, Manila, November 1998, in *Chinese America: History and Perspective 2000* (San Francisco: Chinese Historical Society of America and San Francisco State University, 2000).

7. Chan Heng Chee, *The Dynamics of One-Party Dominance: The PAP at the Grassroots* (Singapore: Singapore University Press, 1976); and Ong Jin Hui, Tong Chee Kiong, and Tan Ern Ser, eds., *Understanding Singapore Society* (Sin-

gapore: Times Academic Press, 1997), essays by Chiew Seen Kong (pp. 86–106) and Chan Heng Chee (pp. 294–306); Leo Suryadinata, ed., *Ethnic Chinese as Southeast Asians* (Singapore: Institute of Southeast Asian Studies, 1997), essay by Lee Kam Hing, pp. 72–107; Loh Kok Wah, *The Politics of Chinese Unity in Malaysia: Reform and Conflict in the Malaysian Chinese Association, 1971–1973*, Occasional Paper no. 70 (Singapore: Maruzen Asia and Institute of Southeast Asian Studies); Wang Gungwu, "The Chinese: What Kind of Minority?" in *China and the Chinese Overseas* (Singapore: Times Academic Press, 1991), pp. 285–302; Wang Gungwu, "Malaysia: Contending Elites" and "Reflections on Malaysian Elites," in *Community and Nation: China, Southeast Asia, and Australia*, new ed. (Sydney: Allen & Unwin, 1992), pp. 197–215, 216–235.

8. Francis L. K. Hsu, *The Challenge of the American Dream: The Chinese in the United States* (Belmont, Calif.: Wadsworth Publishing Co., 1971); Peter Kwong, *Chinatown, N.Y. Labor and Politics, 1930–1950* (New York: Monthly Review Press, 1979); Henry Tsai Shih-shan, "Living in the Shadow of Exclusion," in his *The Chinese Experience in America* (Bloomington: Indiana University Press, 1986), pp. 90–118. For Canada, Edgar Wickberg, ed., *From China to Canada: A History of the Chinese Communities in Canada* (Toronto: McClelland and Stewart, 1982), pts. 3 and 4, pp. 148–271. The bulk of the writings on the Chinese in Australia deal with the nineteenth century. Scholars have begun to pay more attention to the diminishing numbers of Chinese during the first half of the twentieth century. The two volumes by Eric Rolls provide a vivid popular account:

Sojourners: The Epic Story of China's Centuries Old Relationship with Australia, vol. 1, *Flowers and the Wide Sea* (1992) and vol. 2, *Citizens* (1996), both published by the University of Queensland Press, Brisbane. Arthur Huck, *The Chinese in Australia* (Melbourne: Longmans, 1967), is still useful. How Chinese lives were constrained can be found in sections of A. C. Palfreeman, *The Administration of the White Australia Policy* (Melbourne: Melbourne University Press, 1967).

9. Stephen FitzGerald, *China and the Overseas Chinese: A Study of Peking's Changing Policy, 1949–1970* (Cambridge: Cambridge University Press, 1972).

10. When Hong Kong, Taiwan, and mainland Chinese migrate to foreign lands, they join the ranks of the Chinese sojourners or migrants, and many ultimately settle abroad as the Chinese overseas, a part of the Chinese diaspora. But, like those from the mainland, they are not *huaqiao* or "Chinese overseas" when at home in Hong Kong and Taiwan, both accepted as Chinese territory. Numerous writers, especially journalists writing in Western languages, have been confusing and misleading on these two points, because they lump all Chinese outside mainland China together with the Chinese overseas; Wang Gungwu, "Greater China and the Chinese Overseas," in *Greater China: The Next Superpower?* ed. David Shambaugh (Oxford: Oxford University Press, 1995), pp. 274–296. Some do so in ignorance of the meaning of the concept of "overseas Chinese," while others may have a political agenda, notably those who argue that Taiwan is not Chinese territory.

11. Twentieth-century sojourning was supported by increasingly better communications linking ethnic Chinese with developments in China. It was much easier to learn the Chinese language and receive books and periodicals. Films and TV videos and other cultural artifacts could be transported long distances and reach homes in the most remote settlements; Wang Gungwu, "Sojourning: the Chinese Experience in Southeast Asia", in Reid, ed., *Sojourners and Settlers*, pp. 9–14.

12. Wang Gungwu, "Ethnic Chinese: The Past in Their Future."

13. Thomas B. Gold, "Go with Your Feelings: Hong Kong and Taiwan Popular Culture in Greater China," in *Greater China: The Next Superpower?* ed. David Shambaugh (Oxford: Oxford University Press, 1995), pp. 255–273. And L. Ling-chi Wang, "Roots and the Changing Identity of the Chinese in the United States," in *The Living Tree: The Changing Meaning of Being Chinese Today*, ed. Tu Wei-ming (Stanford: Stanford University Press, 1994), pp. 185–212.

14. Wang Gungwu, *China and Southeast Asia: Myths, Threats, and Culture* (Singapore: World Scientific and Singapore University Press, 1999), pp. 14–19.

15. It is really quite remarkable how contradictory Western writers on the Chinese overseas can be. The number of books that mislead their non-Chinese readers about the brilliance of all Chinese entrepreneurs is too many to mention here. At the other end are those who deny that Chinese culture has anything to do with the successes reported, and any

reference to cultural factors is dismissed by them as misguided; one notable example is Rupert Hodder, *Merchant Princes of the East: Cultural Delusions, Economic Success, and the Overseas Chinese in Southeast Asia* (Chichester: John Wiley & Sons, 1996). Yet others confuse the Chinese of Hong Kong and Taiwan with the diaspora Chinese: two otherwise useful studies of this kind are: Constance Lever-Tracy, David Ip, and Noel Tracy, *The Chinese Diaspora and Mainland China: An Emerging Economic Synergy* (New York: St. Martin's Press, 1996), and *Overseas Chinese Business Networks in Asia*, produced by the East Asian Analytical Unit, Department of Foreign Affairs and Trade, Canberra, 1995.

16. The most notoriously misleading figure often quoted is that the Chinese controlled 70 percent of Indonesia's wealth, which is patently untrue. This is sometimes carefully explained as meaning 70 percent of that country's corporate wealth, but how that figure was arrived at is not known. If it includes the large conglomerates and monopolies in which privileged Chinese have prominent shares, it is far from clear what proportions they own and what real control they have as agents of the *pribumi*, or indigenous, cronies of those holding political and military power; Wang Gungwu, *China and Southeast Asia*, pp. 5–14.

17. The children may or may not continue to live in their new homes. For example, many return to work in their original homes while keeping their foreign citizenship. The best-known examples are found among the Hong Kong Chinese; see Ronald Skeldon, ed., *Reluctant Exiles? Migration from Hong Kong and the New Overseas Chinese* (Armonk,

N.Y.: M. E. Sharpe, 1994), where there are examples of their practices in Canada, Australasia, the United States, the United Kingdom, and Singapore.

18. This sentiment emerged nationwide with the warm response to the most successful book of this genre, Richard Bernstein and Ross H. Munro, *The Coming Conflict with China* (New York: Alfred A. Knopf, 1997). Further aggravation has come in the area of national security, with the suspicion that some Chinese Americans might have spied for the People's Republic of China. A more balanced study is Andrew J. Nathan and Robert S. Ross, *The Great Wall and the Empty Fortress: China's Search for Security* (New York: W.W. Norton, 1997).

19. Racial sensitivities toward people of Chinese descent are likely to continue for a long while. Ethnic Chinese are late starters in the lobbying game. For example, when some Chinese Americans raised funds for the Democratic Party in the 1990s, their imperfect grasp of the subtleties involved was compounded by an excess of zeal. While their efforts were accompanied by easy access to the White House, the possible role that Chinese Americans might have played in Sino-American relations suffered a salutary setback as they realized they had much to learn if they wished to play an effective part.

20. Roderick MacFarquhar, *New York Review of Books*, April 1997. Perhaps Deng Xiaoping did understand what the scriptwriters of the television series *Heshang* (River Elegy) were trying to say by attacking China's stubbornly land-bound past and the conservatism that came with it, and

advocating a modern turning to the ocean. Although he was angry with Zhao Ziyang for defending it, he was probably not averse to equating modernity with a seaward and open approach toward the outside world. After all, his economic reforms reflected exactly that perspective; Han Minzhu, with the assistance of Hua Sheng, ed., *Cries for Democracy: Writings and Speeches from the 1989 Chinese Democracy Movement* (Princeton: Princeton University Press, 1990), pp. 20–22.

21. These lectures were delivered three months before the financial crisis began. At the time, there were no signs of such a crisis on the horizon. The dramatic changes in the fortunes of some of the Chinese overseas in Southeast Asia have been much commented on. Some of the issues are discussed in my recent writings (see *China and Southeast Asia* and "Ethnic Chinese"), but it is too early to draw conclusions about the outcome, even though there are now signs of economic recovery in some countries.

22. For a brief account of the efforts of Liao Chengzhi (1908–1983) on behalf of the overseas Chinese, see FitzGerald, *China and the Overseas Chinese*, pp. 172–182, 192–195. See also Wang Gungwu, "External China as a New Policy Area," in *China and the Chinese Overseas*, pp. 222–239.

Index

Acculturation, 83–84
Americas, 22, 57, 61–64, 71, 87, 95
Annan. *See* Vietnam
Arabs, 9, 11, 17, 30
Asia, 2, 25, 61, 85, 94, 107–108, 113
Assimilation, 14, 39–42, 45, 51, 61, 81, 83–84, 87, 94, 98, 112, 116–117
Association of Southeast Asian Nations, 101
Australasia, 57, 61–62, 71, 87, 91, 95, 115
Australia, 41, 61–62, 71, 96–97, 103, 113

Baba. See *Peranakan*
Bali, 34
Bandung Conference, 93
Bangkok, 53
Bans on migration, trade, travel, 24–26, 30, 37, 46–47, 50–51, 57

Batavia, 30–31, 53, 55–56, 58
Beijing, 7, 17, 25, 29, 89, 93, 107–108
Britain, 22, 25, 81, 83, 111, 113
British Malaya, 90
Buddhism, 36, 49
Buddhist(s), 9–10, 57
Burma, 83, 88, 101
Business, 25, 59–60, 81, 90, 98–102, 112, 115. *See also* Trade

California, 62
Cambodia, 8, 19, 34, 50, 83
Canada, 41, 62, 96, 104
Cantonese, 52, 66
Catholicism, 55
Champa, 19, 50
Chinatown, 63, 91
Chinese identity, 31, 64–65, 73, 87, 92–98, 104
Chinese language, 59, 71, 73–75, 85, 98, 106
Chinese mestizo, 55–56, 60, 83

143

Chinese students, 10, 62, 72
Commerce. *See* Business; Trade
Communists, 82, 86, 99, 101
Confucianism. *See* Neo-Confucianism
Continental, earthbound, 3–11, 15–18, 20–22, 26, 30–32, 35–37, 52, 111–112
Coolie, 46, 48, 61, 64–65
Cultural maintenance, 59, 84, 87, 93, 112, 116–117
Cultural Revolution, 113

Deng Xiaoping, 103, 111, 114
Dutch, 25, 28, 30, 34, 52–53, 55, 83, 107

Earthbound. *See* Continental
East Asia, 23, 31, 43, 102
Eastern Europe, 22, 101
Education, 59–60, 62–63, 70, 72–74, 76, 81, 84, 87, 92–93, 96–102, 104
Elites, elite status, 7, 19–20, 44, 47, 56, 81, 88–92
Emigrants. *See* migrant(s)
Eurasians, 75
Europe and the West, 3, 6, 11, 22, 25–26, 95, 97, 102, 105
European migrant(s), 57, 61, 65, 87, 91
Europeans, European powers, 2, 11, 28–29, 33, 41, 45–46, 51–55, 57, 59, 61–62, 64, 69, 75, 81–82

Faifo (Hoi An), 53
Family, 2, 5, 7, 20, 26–27, 33, 35, 44–45, 47, 50, 55–56, 58–59, 61, 63–64, 72, 74, 80–81, 96, 103, 114
Fujian, 13, 23, 25, 27–28, 37, 52, 107, 115
Fujianese. *See* Hokkien
Fuzhou, 12

Germans, 111
Greater China, 107
Guangdong, 5, 8, 13, 20, 23, 25, 27–28, 37, 52, 115
Guangxi, 8, 13
Guangzhou, 6, 8, 10, 13
Guiqiao, 94
Guomindang (Nationalist), 70, 87, 93

Ha-tien, 34
Hainan, 8, 52
Hakka (Kejia), 20, 52
Han (Chinese, empire), 8, 11, 20, 31
Hangzhou, 13, 15, 17
Hoi An. *See* Faifo
Hokkien, 29, 52, 107
Hong Kong, 66, 96, 98, 100, 103, 105, 108, 112, 115–116
Huagong, 47

INDEX

Huaqiao, 7, 47, 52, 54, 65–74, 76–77, 79, 82, 84, 86, 92, 95, 99, 102, 113–114
Huashang, 47

Identity, 34–35, 45, 47, 60, 64–65, 70, 73, 87, 92–98, 104
Immigrants. *See* migrant(s)
Immigration policy, 40–41, 92
India, 9–10, 26, 36, 49, 73
Indian Ocean, 7, 21–22, 26
Indonesia, 89–90, 101, 113
Industrial revolution, 41, 60–61
Integration, 83, 87

Japan, 8, 10, 16, 18, 21, 25, 27–30, 33, 41–42, 51, 66, 71, 85, 102, 107–108, 111–112
Java, 8, 18–19, 34, 45, 50, 55–56, 58
Jews, 57, 75
Jiangsu, 5, 23
Jurchen Jin (dynasty), 15–16

Kaifeng, 7, 15
Kang Youwei, 66
Korea, 10, 16, 29, 42
Kublai Khan, 17–18

Labor migration, 43, 62, 72
Latin America, 41
Lee Kuan Yew, 91
Liang Qichao, 66

Liao Chengzhi, 114
Localization, 88–89, 92

Macau, 28, 31
Mainland China. *See* People's Republic of China
Makassar, 34
Malacca, 25, 34, 53, 58
Malay, 10, 34, 46, 53, 58, 83
Malay Peninsula, 34, 53
Malayan Communist Party, 90
Malaysia, 91, 101, 113
Manchu dynasty, 15, 29, 32–33, 35, 51, 67, 69. *See also* Qing dynasty
Manila, 30–31, 53
Maritime, 3–4, 6, 18–19, 22–25, 28, 30, 32, 37, 52
Marriage. *See* Family
Mediterranean, 1, 6, 11, 22
"Melting pot," 83, 94–95
Merchants. *See* Trade
Mestizo. *See* Chinese mestizo
Migrant(s), 34–35, 39–41, 60–61, 63, 75, 84, 94, 105, 112
Migrant states, 85, 91, 103–104
Migration, 2–5, 19, 34, 40–42, 48–49, 54, 57, 96, 103–106
Ming dynasty, 21–35, 50–51
Minh Huong, 35
Moluccas, 34
Mongols, Yuan dynasty, 16–22, 26, 50

Multiculturalism, 77, 79, 81, 92, 95–97, 99, 104, 117
Muslims, 11, 17, 19, 22, 73, 81

Nagasaki, 31
Nanjing, 13, 48, 74
Nanjing government, 71, 86
Nationalism, 33, 64, 68, 70, 72–76, 79, 85–87, 89–91, 93, 107
Nation-states, 39, 41–42, 82, 88, 94, 116
Native elites, 81, 89, 91
Navy, Naval expeditions, 13, 16, 18, 21, 23, 30
Neo-Confucianism, 20, 26, 33, 44
Netherlands, East Indies, 22–23, 81, 87
North America, 86, 91, 97, 103, 110, 115
Northeast Asia, 110

Opium War, 111
Overseas Chinese. *See Huaqiao*

Patani, 34, 53
Patriotism, 70, 72, 74, 80, 82–84, 86, 92, 95, 99, 102, 114
People's Action Party, 91, 113
People's Republic of China, 94, 96, 98, 100, 103, 106–107
Peranakan, 56–57, 60, 83, 88, 99
Persia, 9, 17, 26

Philippines, 53, 55–56, 83, 88, 101
Ports, 6, 8–10, 18, 25, 28, 34–35, 44–45, 66
Portugal, 22–25, 28, 30

Qing dynasty, 31, 33, 43–45, 52, 66–68
Qiao. See *Huaqiao*

Religion, 9–10, 57, 59–60
Remigration, 95–96, 104, 116
Republic of China, 69–70, 79
Resinicization, 60, 84, 86–87, 92
Revolution, 67, 86, 93
Roman empire, 11
Russia, 110–111

Schools. *See* Education
Science, 97, 102, 104
Shandong, 5, 23
Shanghai, 66, 71, 74
Shipping, 5, 9, 18, 24, 30
Siamese. *See* Thai
Singapore, 90–91, 101, 113
Slavery, 61
Socialism, 82, 101
Sojourners and sojourning, 12, 14, 19, 34–35, 39, 42–44, 46–47, 50–51, 53–59, 61–77, 79–84, 88, 91, 94–96, 98, 100–101, 104–105, 111, 115–117

INDEX

Song dynasty, 13–19, 26, 44, 50, 67
South Asia, 6, 9
South China Sea, 1, 5, 13, 49
South Korea, 109, 112
Southeast Asia, 1–4, 55, 60; development; 6, 8–10; and China, 12, 16, 26–31, 36; Chinese in, 19, 33–34, 75–76, 80–81, 83, 86–88, 91, 99, 108–109; migration/sojourning to, 49–51, 57, 63–65, 67, 71; and trade, 49, 53, 115; and melting pot model, 94–97; modern-day, 101–103, 105
Soviet Union, 101, 109, 111
Spain, 22, 25, 30–31, 34, 52–53, 55, 107
Spanish Philippines, 53
Spratly Islands, 107
Straits Chinese, 83, 91
Suharto, 89, 113
Sumatra, 8, 19, 50
Sun Yat-sen, 66, 68, 70, 114

Taipei, 89, 93
Taiwan, 28, 31–32, 51, 86, 93, 96, 98, 100, 103, 109, 112
Tang dynasty, 1, 10–12, 20
Taoist, 57
Tengku Abdul Rahman, 93
Teochiu, 52

Thai, 34, 36, 83, 89, 101
Trade, 1–2, 5–9, 11–19, 21–34, 36–37, 47–51, 53, 56, 59–60, 62, 82, 89. *See also* Business
Tribute, 8, 21, 24, 36

United Malay National Organization, 113
United Nations, 82
United States, 41, 62, 72, 83, 94–96, 102–103, 109–112
Universities, 71–72, 74, 102

Victoria (Australia), 62
Vietnam, 5–6, 8, 13–14, 19, 33–35, 42, 50, 53, 83, 88, 101, 113

Waiji huaren, 94
Wako (pirates), 21, 27–28
West. *See* Europe and the West
West Asia, 6, 9
West Borneo, 34
Women, 57–60, 63. *See also* Family
World War II, 73, 77, 88, 101, 105

Xinke, sinkeh, 60
Xu Fu, 8

Yangzi (river, valley), 4, 5, 13, 27, 48
Yongle, emperor, 21

Yuan. *See* Mongols, Yuan dynasty
Yue (Hundred, peoples), 5

Zhejiang, 5, 13, 23, 37
Zheng Chenggong (Koxinga), 28, 32, 34, 51

Zheng He, 21, 23–24
Zhenla, 8, 50
Zhou Enlai, 95
Zhu Xi, 20, 33
Zhu Yuanzhang, 21